MOVE TO THE EDGE, DECLARE IT CENTER

MOVE TO THE EDGE, DECLARE IT CENTER

Practices and Processes for **Creatively** Solving Complex Problems

EVERETT **HARPER**

WILEY

For general information on our other products and services or for technical support, please contact our Customer Care Department within the United States at (800) 762-2974, outside the United States at (317) 572-3993 or fax (317) 572-4002.

Wiley publishes in a variety of print and electronic formats and by print-on-demand. Some material included with standard print versions of this book may not be included in e-books or in print-on-demand. If this book refers to media such as a CD or DVD that is not included in the version you purchased, you may download this material at http://booksupport.wiley.com. For more information about Wiley products, visit www.wiley.com.

Library of Congress Cataloging-in-Publication Data is Available:

ISBN 9781119849889 (Hardcover)
ISBN 9781119849902 (ePDF)
ISBN 9781119849896 (ePub)

COVER DESIGN: PAUL MCCARTHY

SKY10032383_012922

To Jacqueline Harper – I'm here because you keep stepping into the unknown with curiosity, enthusiasm and purpose. You embody the spirit of Move to the Edge, Declare It Center, and I'm grateful to have you as a model.

Contents

Acknowledgments

To Steve Broback and Jason Preston, you invited me on stage to present the earliest glimmer of this work in 2017 at the Dent the Future Conference, and I appreciate your generosity and curiosity. Cris Beasely for making the connection. Shout-out to Dave Whorton, Maria Hilton, and the Tugboat Conference for helping me get pragmatic in 2021.

To the many people who read early drafts of this book and provided great feedback: Ben Hecht, Roberta Katz, Morgan Webb, Daria Walls Torres, Ken Lynch, Erin Worsham, Shannon Arvizu, Molly Tapias, Cheryl Contee, Jenifer Fuqua, Kurt Foeller, Sarah Israel, Ed Batista, Matt Hammer, Melinda Byerly, Kristin Smith, Neil Cohen, and especially Muema Loembe.

To the connectors – my imaginal cells sharing their insights, contacts, and enthusiasm: Adam Grant, Mitaly Chakraborty, Margaret Greenberg, Jareau Wade, Leslie Mallman, Lili Root, Monica Guzman, Nicole Jarbo, Judy Wade, Tim Brown, Cris Beasely, Carlee Gomes, Laura Delizonna, Prof. Damon Phillips, Ellen Leanse, Deb Cohan, Leigh Morgan, Damon Brown, and Ellen McGirt. Flowers for the irrepressible Shaherose Charania – without you, none of this would be possible. Special shout-out to Monica Byrne – you've been inspiring me for 30 years, from side-eye to the Anti-Resume.

To the leaders who agreed to share their experiences for this book: Jana, Danielle, Nate Mook, Jen Pahlka, Abdul Smith. You brought this book to life.

To the readers of late drafts, so much appreciation for your sharp eyes, and occasionally sharp tongues, in order to make this book better: Caroline Lambert, Andre Natta, Stewart Ugelow, Tiffani Ashley Bell, Kelly Werner, and especially Jen Tress for your consistent insight on writing. Special shout-out to Anthony Grant, for your insightful imagery that gives readers memorable visual guideposts to follow.

To the Trussels – past and present employees of Truss – whose insight, creativity, and desire to make a positive impact in the world propels so many of the methods and processes in this book. I hope I've represented you well.

To my fellow Dukie, Laura Yorke, for your enthusiasm and laser-sharp viewpoints. You don't suffer fools, and I feel fortunate to make the cut.

To Christina Harbridge, mentor and friend. Am I your favorite yet?

To Mark Ferlatte and Jennifer Leech. How did we do this Truss thing, anyway? Writing this book was an amazing review of all that we've done together, and I'm deeply thankful for your integrity, talent, trust, taste in bourbon, and especially your commitment to values. It's hard to believe those values we wrote together as a tiny startup still hold a company of 130 people together.

To Mei Mei Fox – we met over foie gras cotton candy, bonded over favorite yoga teachers, and have witnessed each other's triumphs and losses. You've been a guide for life, and now for this book. Namaste, girlll.

To Michele Turner, your divine inkwell guided my words when I needed them most.

To Julie Mikuta, for your fierce dedication to justice, and for being an amazing partner in sustaining a vision for a coparenting family. Next book?

To Damiana, I can't wait for you to blow this book out of the water – you are capable of that and more. Amo muito, querida.

To Abby, I couldn't have gotten more fortunate to write a book while being trapped during a pandemic in a house with the best "hype man," teenage whisperer, English teacher editor, and unequivocal supporter. Your spirit and intelligence echo in these pages.

About the Author

Everett is the CEO and co-founder of Truss, a human-centered software development company, named as an *Inc 5000* fastest-growing private company in 2020 and 2021. He has led a purpose-driven, impactful, innovative company that's been remote-first since 2011, salary-transparent since 2017, and a diverse workforce that far exceeds standards for technology companies.

He is a rare combination: a Black entrepreneur, with bio-medical and electrical engineering degrees from Duke, an MBA and M.Ed. from Stanford, Silicon Valley startup pedigree, and management consulting at Bain. He has leveraged those experiences into a long track record for solving complex problems with social impact for millions of people, from helping fix Healthcare.gov, community development finance at Self-Help, to fighting global poverty as a board member of CARE.

Everett has a history of firsts: first in his family to college and the first to win a soccer NCAA National Championship for Duke University. He was inducted into the North Carolina Soccer Hall of Fame in 2019.

Everett's distinctive voice and unique history make him a sought-after speaker on DEI, technology startups, leadership, remote/hybrid work, and social entrepreneurship. He has been featured at conferences such as Dent, Tugboat, TechStars, and

Velocity, and on podcasts like the Commonwealth Club and AfroTech. He has written for *Forbes*, *Thrive Global*, and *TechCrunch*. *Move to the Edge, Declare It Center* is his first book.

Everett grew up a small-town kid in New York's Hudson Valley. He currently lives in Oakland, California, making limoncello when life hands him lemons.

Preface

July 7, 2016: Stand Up, Speak Up

I was reading a post by Ellen McGirt,[1] senior editor at *Fortune* magazine, called, "Why Employers Need to Talk about Shootings of Black People,"[2] after 24 hours of drifting in waves of despair about the murders of Alton Sterling and Philando Castile. Her article highlighted the need for employers to go beyond the idea of inclusion to the more resonant emotion of compassion. She argued that when two Black men are killed by police, one at a traffic stop in front of his four-year-old daughter, employers must recognize that their employees, like much of the rest of the country, are likely to be deeply affected. I nodded my head with her clear, fierce, call to employers to go beyond their comfort zone.

And then I realized: "*I'm* the employer."

I'm the CEO of Truss, a highly diverse, remote-first software development company. My cofounders and I worked hard to make our company inclusive, using "radical candor"[3] to address issues that many companies avoid. But news of these murders required more of me. First, as a Black man, I felt unmoored and vulnerable. There is no sign on my car nor a logo on my jacket that reads, "Don't shoot, I'm a CEO." At the same time, part of my job as a CEO is to set a foundation so our employees can continue to do great work. My silence would be turning away from that responsibility. I needed to write a speech that acknowledged that while I'm a leader . . . I'm also a target.

This is what I wrote that afternoon to the Trussels, our employees.

Many of my friends are "calling in Black today." Much respect. For those who can't or who choose not to, it's a hard, hard day to grapple with two police murders of Black men while still maintaining our professional demeanor and standards of excellence. (Note: We do that every day. Today is harder.)

If you have a work colleague who is Black, or who is connected deeply to these shootings, please read Ellen's article. We're all "whole people," and understanding how trauma affects work can make this a better company for everyone.

We can't have the benefits of a diverse and vibrant company without acknowledging when it gets hard. Today is one of those days for me, and "as an employer," it feels awkward, challenging – and necessary – to address it. Personally, I'm exhausted, so I'm not up for engaging in conversation. But I **can** create a tone and a space where Trussels can engage without fear of reprisal, toxicity, or indifference.

Let it be so. However you choose to engage, at minimum read Ellen's article, take a moment to reflect, and take care of each other.

This was one a moment when I moved to my edge, when I had to step into the unknown, feeling uncertain, and decide how to address a complex issue. I suspect you have encountered this moment too, like the other leaders you will read about in this book. What you will learn is how to stand up, speak up, and move forward anyway. You will learn how to practice, so when the moment comes, you are centered and ready to provide the leadership your team, company and our communities need.

Introduction

Once in a generation, there is an event that fractures our experience. The summer of 2020 offered three: protests against racial injustice, massive forest fires in the western United States, and a worldwide pandemic. We can't unsee the knee on George Floyd's neck, supernatural orange-smoke skies, or the faces of intubated elders dying of COVID alone.

Many of us had to respond to these unprecedented events and make decisions without guidelines or playbooks. Should we ask people to keep working while they're at risk of exposure to COVID? How do we support our teammates during the workday, while they are simultaneously acting as elementary school teachers to their children? Let's be honest – how many of us froze when we didn't know the answer to those questions? I know I did.

We're all susceptible to these responses. Some are rooted in neurochemistry – the well-known flight-or-fight response. But others are rooted in our inherited leadership and management models, based on nineteenth-century factories, where systems were well understood and problems had a singular "right answer." We've been rewarded since kindergarten for raising our hand first with the right answer, preparing us to be "decisive" adult leaders.

But twenty-first-century problems like racial injustice, climate change, and pandemics are complex. The key property of complex systems is that they are not well understood, there are many unknowns, and problems often do not have a singular right answer. As a result, there is the risk of causing unintended harm. In short, the nineteenth-century management model is a mismatch for today's leaders navigating complex systems. Many of us know it.

In the early stages of the COVID pandemic, as we realized that the impact was not measured in weeks, but months, I compared strategies with highly experienced, successful leaders. Out of the public spotlight, they were anxious and flummoxed, and they finally admitted, with grief and exhaustion, "I don't know what to do. I don't know what to say. I don't have the right answer." The fissures that opened this decade are a vivid wake-up call that the "new normal" is complex, and we need new mindsets, processes, and practices to match.

Move to the Edge, Declare It Center is a framework to help leaders of organizations and teams navigate through complex problems when they don't know the "right" answer and there's no predetermined plan, playbook, or procedure. Move to the Edge is a set of practices, processes, and infrastructure to address complex problems, and Declare It Center is a set of methods to systematize, scale, share, and sustain the best approaches throughout an organization.

This book emerges from two distinct sources. First, from my experience as CEO and co-founder of my company, Truss. Since 2011, we have developed human-centered software to help our clients navigate complex, global, consequential problems, from helping to fix Healthcare.gov to modernizing supply chain and delivery logistics systems for some of the largest organizations in the world. We built a company that's been remote-first for over a decade, exceeds our industry in diversity and inclusion, and is anchored by a values-driven culture that helped us stay connected through the pandemic.

The second source is a lifetime of being on the edge, navigating the pursuit of excellence from the distinct vantage point of being an outsider. While I have a history of firsts – first in my family to college, first NCAA National Champion in any sport for Duke University – as a Black man in the United States, those firsts do not protect me from being a target of racial violence and discrimination. Every "routine" traffic stop has the potential for a deadly outcome, and despite being the keynote speaker at the TechStars startup conference, I was singled out by an armed security guard at the entrance, "Do you belong here?"

For me and other outsiders, navigating uncertainty is first a survival skill, then an expertise, and finally a gift. But it comes at a cost – the pressure and weight can deplete one's energy and lead to burnout. To avoid this, I've centered on different Interior Practices to prepare me for making high-stakes decisions under stress. In uncertain times with complex problems, leaders need Interior Practices as a companion for their Exterior (organizational) Practices. *Move to the Edge, Declare It Center* is a framework that integrates both, and I will share these practices in depth throughout this book.

We're living in a new normal. We have urgent, complex challenges to address, and twentieth-century tools don't work for twenty-first-century problems. Leaders need to approach today's complex systems with a different mindset – led by curiosity and experimentation – while building systems to scale, share, and sustain their best solutions. *Move to the Edge, Declare It Center* is a framework of exterior and interior practices that will enable you to make better decisions under uncertainty and complexity.

Two Kinds of Problems: Complicated and Complex

One of the key contributions to our understanding of complex systems comes from the Santa Fe Institute, a nonprofit research institute, using direct observation and mathematical modeling to explain important phenomena. In particular, categorizing problems as *complex* versus *complicated* helps to explain why some of our approaches to problem solving can make things worse.

Complicated Problems

Complicated problems consist of elements whose behaviors and interactions are more well-understood, often linear, and therefore predictable. For example, let's say you want to build a passenger jet. If you have a plan, hire expert designers, gather builders, and have enough money, you'll probably succeed in building a jet. Even though building a jet is neither simple nor cheap, the relationships between all the parts and labor are well understood. When there is a complicated problem to solve, such as how to reduce the cost of making a jet, the best approach is to optimize those predictable relationships. Sourcing the same rotor from a cheaper supplier, standardizing quality measurements, or negotiating for lower labor wages are logical approaches to solving the complicated problem of reducing costs. Great operational leaders focus on building with efficient, measurable, repeatable execution.

This is an advanced version of a model that emerged out of Fredrick Taylor's scientific management in the late nineteenth century.[1] Taylor did "time and motion" studies of workers in factories, creating scientific models that included workers as part of the equation. The promise was that one could develop a scientific equation with a right answer, enabling managers and owners to operate factories in predictable, measurable ways. Eventually known as *Taylorism*, this approach to measuring production ushered in the assembly-line system used to manufacture goods in the early twentieth century. Over the next hundred years, it influenced all sorts of work, from retail to software production. As this became more widespread, military leaders, business schools, and management consultants developed operational and leadership models of productivity to accompany Taylor's approach. The command-control, optimize and execute, hierarchical organizational models derived from the understanding of problems as complicated. There *was* a right answer, and the most admired leaders had it.

Taylorism produced some obvious fallacies, especially with the rise of professions where people were paid primarily to think, as opposed to assemble. The shift to *knowledge work* made using complicated methods like time-and-motion equations to judge productivity less useful. For example, it's hard to imagine that the effectiveness of the famous 1959 "Think Small" Volkswagen Beetle advertising campaign[2] could have been calculated with a linear productivity equation that measured words per copywriter. Other fields, from management consulting, to design, computer science, and software development, defied previously valid assessments of productivity, quality, or value, based on Taylor's time-and-motion models.

Think small.

Our little car isn't so much of a novelty
any more.
    A couple of dozen college kids don't
try to squeeze inside it.
    The guy at the gas station doesn't ask
where the gas goes.
    Nobody even stares at our shape.
    In fact, some people who drive our little

flivver don't even think 32 miles to the gallon is going any great guns.
    Or using five pints of oil instead of five
quarts.
    Or never needing anti-freeze.
    Or racking up 40,000 miles on a set of
tires.
    That's because once you get used to

some of our economies, you don't even
think about them any more.
    Except when you squeeze into a small
parking spot. Or renew your small insurance. Or pay a small repair bill.
    Or trade in your old VW for a
new one.
    Think it over.

1959 "Think Small" Volkswagen Beetle advertising campaign
*Source: Bill Bernbach's iconic 'Think Small' Volkswagen Beetle ad. Martin
Schilder Groep/Flickr, CC BY-NC-SA*

Early in my career, I was advised to come early to the office
and stay late, not because it would produce better work but
because I would be regarded as a highly productive, committed,
hard worker. I watched colleagues walk the halls, wearing their

"I'm working hard" face, coincidentally timed for their manager to see them as they arrived at the office. Today, part of the debate about working from home versus returning to the office is framed as, "How do I know my employees are working?" This leads to misplaced choices like measuring how long employees are at their computers or in virtual meetings, instead of measuring the outcomes of their work. This is a manifestation of the complicated model of productivity, where there is a linear relationship between time in office and "This is good" work. In contrast, what is now being considered as "the future of work" is that global, hybrid, knowledge work doesn't assume a building – it enables us to think in new ways about defining work with purpose and impact.

Complex Problems

Complex problems consist of elements that are distinct from *complicated* problems. Samuel Arbesman, a complexity scientist, declares, "Complex is a large number of moving parts interacting in multifaceted ways."[3] The interactions are less well understood, and the relationships are often nonlinear. Because the elements are interacting in multifaceted ways, you can't necessarily predict what the results of those interactions are going to be.

Peter Ho is chairman of the Urban Redevelopment Authority in Singapore. His expertise on complexity informed his country's response to the threat of SARS in 2003, and he wrote:

> The natural world is complex. In comparison, an engineering system – be it an airplane or a telecommunications satellite – is merely complicated.[4]

A complex system does not necessarily behave in a repeatable and predetermined manner. As a result, not only may a change to one part of a complex system yield unexpected results, but these results may be hidden. Think of the impact on your commute time of an accident just before a merge into a tunnel. Not only is the main route clogged, but so are the side routes and your secret cut-throughs. Further, impatient drivers might start to take more risks, driving on the shoulders or swerving to jump lanes and causing new accidents. Many of these effects are out of your view, but they have significant impact on whether you arrive on time to your first meeting. Whether it is the complex queuing systems you rely on to get to work on time or the global supply chain, unexpected changes are difficult to plan for because of the sheer number of elements interacting in unpredictable ways.

Twentieth-century problems were, by and large, understood as complicated. I believe that our most urgent twenty-first-century problems are complex (Figure I.1). The problem is when a leader tries to address a complex problem with an approach designed for a complicated problem (Figure I.2).

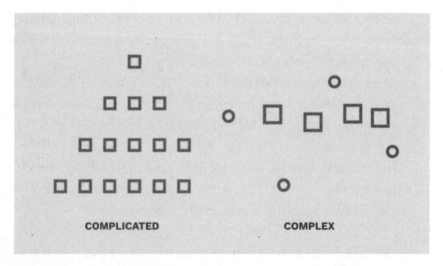

COMPLICATED   COMPLEX

FIGURE I.1 Complicated vs. complex systems: Elements only.
Source: Everett Harper and Josh Franklin, 2021.

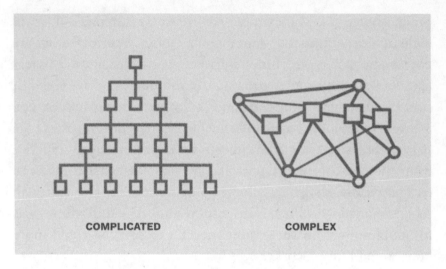

FIGURE I.2 Complicated vs. complex systems: Impact of adding one new element on relationships.
Source: Everett Harper and Josh Franklin, 2021.

The Mismatch

When we apply complicated problem solving to complex problems, there's bound to be a mismatch. For example, problem solving in a complicated system is often about *optimization*, where the goal is to fine-tune a process to reduce wasted time, materials, errors, or friction, while achieving the same outcome. For example, if I want to ensure I get exercise before going to work, I set my alarm, prep my water bottles, and lay out my workout clothes before going to bed. These are steps to *optimize* my system and reduce the likelihood that I will hit the snooze button.[5]

Returning to the example of building a plane, once a builder understands the relationships between the elements, from parts, to suppliers, to builders, then the focus is appropriately on building systems to optimize different factors in construction. The focus on becoming efficient saves millions of dollars, and so very sophisticated systems manage these relationships. The key is the valid, tested knowledge of the interactions between each of the elements in the system.

In contrast, complexity affects many industries, but I will focus on an industry where I am most familiar: software development. At one time, software was considered a linear process with well-understood inputs and outputs. As a result, it could be managed using the same Taylor-derived principles. The Waterfall method, named after the Gantt chart of successive blue bars of tasks stretched over a linear calendar, was the best practice from the days of mainframes. It gave managers the comfort of prediction, and a stick to enforce compliance when the Waterfall schedule went off-kilter.[6] The response to missed deadlines was to double down on the easiest variable to control – add more hours or add more workers.

There are two significant assumptions in this methodology that do not account for complexity.[7] The first assumption is that the relationship between those elements is correct. The second assumption is that there aren't any other factors affecting the system. Add a factor – you just hired three new engineers who are still learning, your code becomes noncompliant due to a new regulation, or your customer needs a new feature to keep up with a competitor's latest release – and it throws the system completely off.[8] The project becomes horribly late, way over budget, or is delivered to a customer who rejects it. As engineering leader Leslie Miley told me, "Systems can either be complicated or complex, with the latter exhibiting nondeterministic [unpredictable] behavior. If your system is exhibiting the latter, Perhaps it's time to rethink."

In software development, one of the most influential responses to the unknown and unexpected of complex systems was iterative development, commonly referred to as "Agile." Agile refers to the Agile Manifesto, developed over three days in 2001 by 17 industry thinkers and practitioners.[9] Among many declarations, two of the key principles are "Individuals and interactions, over processes and tools" and "Responding to change, over following a plan," which is further elaborated as "Welcome changing requirements, even late in development."

Over the next 20 years, this framework has been adopted, adapted, codified, and, most importantly, shown to deliver value, especially in complex systems.[10] Putting people-first while welcoming the unexpected is a powerful prescription in uncertain times with complex problems. It is no accident that these processes emerged at the same time that computing power was rapidly increasing in complexity, both in terms of scale and impact. Lean Startup extended the same type of thinking into the innovation and entrepreneur communities, bringing an explicit perspective of learning like a scientist into the creation of software, business models, and companies.[11]

Even organizations that embodied formal hierarchy – often called command-control – experienced the shift in leadership models and frameworks. For example, in *Team of Teams*, General Stanley McCrystal documents how the old centralized strategic model was repeatedly failing in Iraq.[12] The Iraqis were more agile and consistently stymied the progress of his forces. Rather than adding more forces and more weapons, he shifted his model to allow different military units to create experiments, to engage enemy forces in their own way and evolve their local knowledge. He invested in communication systems to accelerate rapid feedback, and to spread successful experiments to other troops. It was this shift that enabled his forces to make significant progress. The principles of agility, communication, iteration, experiments, and rapid feedback are core practices to deal with complexity, uncertainty, and unknowns.

In sum, we've inherited models of management, leadership, and performance that are based on the assumption that systems are complicated, we can predict how the elements in the system will interact, and there is a "right answer." Unfortunately, this assumption is not effective in an era of increasing complexity, unpredictable elements, and diverse global stakeholders. The good news is that we can use a new framework to address complex issues and make better decisions, despite lots of unknowns and uncertainties. Let me introduce a story about one complex issue – diversity, inclusion, and equal pay – and our approach to addressing it using the core practices in Move to the Edge, Declare It Center.

Case Study: Introducing Salary Transparency

Imagine your first day at work, and your business card looks like this:

What would you think? Might you wonder, "Does everybody have their salaries displayed on their business card?" Might you look around and ask yourself, "How do I compare with the other directors?" I suspect you are definitely thinking, "Why on earth would a company do this?"

While we don't have our salaries on our business cards, we did make all salaries transparent in 2017. Why? We wanted to solve a complex problem: racial and gender inequality in compensation. In most labor markets, BIPOC[13] people and people who identify with she/her pronouns get paid less than White men for the same job. It is an old, persistent problem, but we treated it as an obstacle we needed to overcome in order to build the diverse, inclusive company we wanted. There weren't many companies to emulate, and we couldn't find any that were doing it explicitly for diversity, equity, and inclusion (DEI) purposes. We were on the edge.

Truss was founded with 67 percent "underrepresented minorities."[14] Our founding team of me – a Black male CEO – and a technical leadership team of a White woman COO and White male CTO was absolutely contrary to the Silicon Valley startup narrative in 2011. Despite degrees from Duke, Stanford, University of California (UC)–Santa Cruz and UC–Berkeley, recognized engineering expertise in pioneering technical practices, and brand recognition from a "hot" company, we were the "anti-pattern." The desirable startup teams in 2011 were young, White, male engineers from prestige programs. We were definitely outsiders . . . and that gave us an important insight. From our vantage point, we could see the flaws in the assumed benefit of homogeneous teams, and we could access networks of knowledge and talent that were ignored by the mainstream of Silicon Valley. That didn't guarantee success, however – we had to turn our advantage into a sustainable company.

Our Move to the Edge started with several hypotheses:

- Building a diverse company is a long series of investments resulting in a network of trust.
- Diverse teams outperform nondiverse teams, especially around innovation, decision-making, and accounting for risks.

- Diversity and inclusion initiatives must be central to the core operating model of the company. DEI initiatives that are only marketing or human resource initiatives will fail.

- There are skilled, motivated, and high-integrity people from diverse backgrounds who live outside the San Francisco Bay area.

Those were our beliefs – now we had to test them with data. I started writing articles on using networks to find diverse candidates, in order to attract like-minded employees. I found research from academics like Dr. Kathy Williams,[16] demonstrating that companies with diverse boards and executive teams outperform nondiverse ones on a variety of metrics, including stock price valuation on the public markets.[17] We built a network of relationships by attending dozens of events, meetups, and gatherings focused on diversity and inclusion, and learned how we could help one another. I joined a new group called Black Founders and helped start the N.O.D., a social gathering for Black men in tech, finance, and legal fields.

Each of these actions was small, but we followed a principle of improving by marginal gains. We gained insights that validated or invalidated these hypotheses. Over time, we felt more equipped to place bigger bets and make bigger commitments. In 2016, we joined the first startup cohort of Project Include, a data-driven DEI initiative anchored at the Kapor Center.[18] We validated that DEI initiatives weren't successful as just HR or marketing initiatives. We sharpened our perspective, learning that the best results come when the CEO is directly involved, either hands-on or as an executive sponsor. Cultural change requires the CEO to set, model, and reinforce purpose and accountability.

Finally, there was the well-documented, cross-industry data on pay disparities. We surmised that if there is a pay disparity between a Black woman and a White man hired on the same day for the same job, they could perform equally well, earn the same percentage salary increase, yet in five years, have a substantial difference in their compensation. How long do you think that high-performing Black woman will remain at your company after she finds out that she is being paid less for the same job? We saw that even well-intentioned companies fell into that trap. If we wanted to attract and retain people from diverse backgrounds at Truss, we believed salary transparency was a concrete initiative to address this complex problem.

But we didn't know the answer, so we started on the journey using what became the framework for Move to the Edge, Declare It Center. I'll return to the specific methods in the Salary Transparency Case Study in Chapter 2. However, it is time to examine the ways we can make poor decisions around complex problems, despite our best intentions.

Defeating the Defaults: Making Decisions Under Uncertainty

When I wrote the July 2016 letter that opened the book, I was struggling with two significant issues: complexity and uncertainty. The issue of racial justice is complex, and I felt deeply uncertain about how to address it with my company. My "I don't know" moment was how my employees and the larger public would respond as I revealed how vulnerable I felt. There were significant risks if I got the message wrong or created unintended consequences. I decided to show up and speak up, and my message resonated – not just with my employees but also with a larger readership when I published it in *Forbes*. I've also witnessed leaders, including myself, making poor decisions when confronted with complexity and uncertainty, especially during the summer of 2020. I got curious about how complexity and uncertainty affects decision-making, and it became an important building block for the Move the Edge, Declare It Center framework.

If you searched "decision-making under uncertainty" on the internet, you would find thousands of academic citations across the fields of organizational behavior, neuroscience, behavioral economics, and computer science. In addition to the academic work, the topic shows up in the theater (from *Hamlet* to *Hamilton*) and even in your decision about which line to get in at the grocery. Suffice to say that a full literature review is way beyond the scope of my brain, your attention, and this book.

Over the course of my career, I have experimented with diverse research, tools, and practices in order to solve complex problems under uncertainty. I learned, through good and bad decisions, to cultivate reliable practices that help make better – though not perfect – decisions in uncertain times. There are four key principles that anchor these practices, and they animate the rest of this book.

Our Brains: Wired for Shortcuts

The first three principles have to do with our brains. First, we're less rational than we think. I used to have endless arguments with economists in grad school, where the dominant paradigm was based on the assumption that humans are rational actors. In contrast, my personal experience reflected theories in social psychology that people use simplifying shortcuts, social cues, and responses to their own emotional states in order to make decisions that might be considered *irrational*. For example, the collected works of Daniel Kahneman and Amos Tversky, detailed in *Thinking, Fast and Slow*, not only begat the field of behavioral economics and won Kahneman a Nobel Prize but also opened the door to more accurate ways of thinking about decision-making that assume that humans are full of predictable biases, illusions, and preferences.

Second, our brains are wired to make systematic shortcuts in decision-making. Kahneman distinguishes two types: System 1 and System 2 thinking. System 1 thinking is *fast*.[19] It's generally unconscious, automatic, and effortless. The brain in System 1 mode assesses the situation, acts without conscious control, and responds. Roughly 98 percent of our thinking occurs here. System 2, on the other hand, is *slow*. It is conscious, deliberate, requires effort, and is rational. The brain in System 2 mode seeks anomalies, missing information and consciously makes decisions – 2 percent of our thinking occurs here. This is purposeful – imagine having to think about contracting and lowering our diaphragm in order to inhale every single breath.[20]

Unfortunately, System 1 (fast) can interfere with or influence System 2 (slow) with numerous cognitive biases without our conscious knowledge. For example, confirmation bias is the tendency to search, interpret, and recall information that confirms one's prior beliefs or preconceptions.[21] For example, a 2021 study of soccer commentators showed that they are six times more likely to associate attributes of physical power to players of darker skin tone than to lighter skin tone.[22] This is an example of how the stereotype that darker-skinned people have greater physical prowess and lack intellectual prowess manifests in everyday, unconscious ways. Confirmation bias shows up in how we assess job candidates as well as how we evaluate business proposals. After all, when 98 percent of our thinking is System 1(fast), we are subject to it unless we consciously slow it down or create systems to help.

The third influence on decision-making relevant for this book is Type 1 and Type 2 decision-making. It's a framework that categorizes different kinds of decisions and can help corral the best of our brainpower to make good decisions. Type 1 decisions are irreversible; Type 2 decisions are reversible. It is crucial to distinguish which type before committing to an action.

For example, if a decision is Type 1 (irreversible) and consequential, rigorously gather facts and perspective from multiple, diverse sources, and actively mitigate risk. On the other hand, that's way too much effort for a reversible Type 2 decision. Instead, it's better to decide quickly, especially if you can do an experiment.

I learned a useful twist to decision-making when listening to author Jim Collins talk about his research with Morten Hansen on the impact of time and risk.[23] They learned that the best decision makers could assess when the risk would increase. For Type 1 decisions that were irreversible and consequential, they would use the best available information and make a decision fast. If risk wasn't going to change for a long time, they would rigorously gather data (see Figure I.3).

I experienced this in my own life. When my father was diagnosed with stomach cancer in 2010, he had multiple treatment options, but he had time to decide which option to

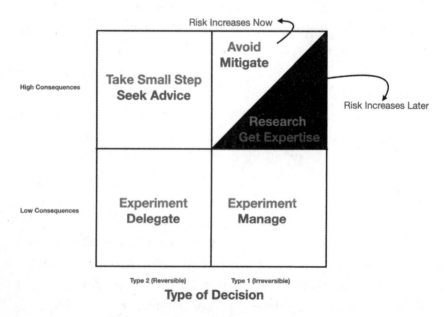

FIGURE I.3   Type 1 versus Type 2 decisions.

pursue before the tumor grew too big and limited his choices. We rigorously sought new data from different doctors, researchers, and other patients. We decided to remove his stomach because we were absolutely clear it was the best choice. It was a Type 1 irreversible decision, but the risk was not increasing rapidly. In contrast, when the Tubbs Fire erupted in 2017 in rural northern California near Calistoga, risk was increasing by the second because of 70 mph wind gusts and dry grasses due to drought. "Evacuate!" was a Type 1 irreversible decision with no time, and it was the right call.

However, there's an interesting development to that story. In Chapter 3, I profile a volunteer disaster response leader who was involved in the 2017 season of California wildfires. In that year, the size, speed, and scale of the fires was so great that it quickly overwhelmed the normal emergency systems. For residents, there was chaos, because the established, reliable system for communication, exit protocols, and shelter infrastructure was insufficient for the complexity of a wildfire at that scale. One of the insights that responders had between 2017 and 2018 was that they had to evolve their perspective from a wildfire as a singular event to a wildfire *season*. In the subsequent years, as police, firefighters, public agencies, and emergency response teams reconceived their systems around a fire season, they developed protocols and training so that residents could be more informed and prepared.[24]

So how did that affect Type 1 decision-making? I got an unexpected perspective from a friend who lives in Santa Rosa, one of the towns that was partially destroyed by those 2017 fires. She said that now when the local emergency air horn sounds, it's actually a comfort. They have prestocked emergency bags, everyone in the house has practiced their routines, and there are clear directions about where to go. They've built a system to respond to a Type 1 (irreversible) decision, and they've developed a routine to train the System 1 (fast) thinking brain so actions are automatic and life-saving instead of chaotic, confusing, and potentially fatal. The theme of encountering a complex problem (wildfires at scale), changing one's perspective (wildfire season), responding with experiments (new protocols), and building infrastructure to make decisions easier (emergency routines) is a sequence that is core to the Move to the Edge, Declare It Center framework.

In summary, we humans are less rational than we believe, we are wired to create mental shortcuts that can lead to biased decisions, and we have to pay attention to whether decisions are reversible and when risk changes. The best we can do – which can become pretty good with practice – is to be aware of these influences, then design habits, practices, and systems to mitigate them. However, all the theory in the world can't save you if your brain is hijacked by neurochemicals screaming, "Run away!" That brings us to the fourth principle: the reactions to stress.

Our Bodies: Reacting to Stress

The COVID pandemic provided a vivid lens to observe common patterns of stress reactions that often lead to poor decision making. I'm sure we have all felt many, if not all of the following list.

- We **freeze**, delaying decisions out of fear of doing the wrong thing.
- We go into **flight**, failing to confront reality, ignoring, minimizing, failing to gather facts that might challenge our belief about the crisis.
- We go into **fight** mode, defending or blaming without thinking, often doing more collateral damage.

- We go into **friend/fawn** mode, soothing our uncertainty by taking actions to make sure we are liked and appreciated by others, instead of making decisions that we fear will make us unpopular – even if it's the right call.

- We return to the **familiar** – the old decision-making models, playbooks, intuitions, or people, ignoring or failing to see that the context has changed and new rules apply.

During my research for this book, I learned about another perspective to these stress patterns, emerging from the work of Shelley Taylor. She noted that the original research of fight-or-flight by Walter Cannon was tested only on men and male animals.[25] Taylor's own experience suggested that women reacted to stress differently, so she replicated the research on female animals and women, and observed distinct patterns.[26] She called the response *tend and befriend*, referring to the nurturing patterns that promote safety, and the creation and maintenance of social networks. These patterns were linked to physiological responses to stress, expanding on Cannon's findings from the last century. It's a compelling argument, and activating social networks is a behavior pattern of multiple leaders profiled in this book. It animates the Imaginal Cells section in Chapter 4.

We're all susceptible to these stress patterns.[27] Some of these are deeply rooted in our neurochemistry; others are the result of repeated training. I am just as likely to make poor decisions even though I am aware of these stress patterns. In this era of uncertainty, we are particularly prone to these mistakes.

For example, I had a conversation in August 2020 with a faculty member at a university who recounted a COVID response town hall led by the school administrators. The university administration decided to shut down the facility, banned access to the school for faculty, and insisted all classes be conducted online. Her medical specialty requires a certain amount of in-person interaction and training for her students. She asked me, "What if you brought in your child for a life-saving procedure and learned that the nurse had never put an IV into a live person, but had only trained on a virtual screen? How much confidence would you have in that nurse?"

When the faculty questioned the decision, the administrators cited the cost of COVID-related sanitization and claimed other schools were doing the same. A quick-witted faculty member did a Google search that revealed other nearby schools were planning to open, using a split schedule and limited hours to accommodate demand. The administrators were surprised, and then my friend realized: "They have no idea. They don't have a plan." They froze instead of having a plan, then defaulted into the familiar – shut down everything until everything is back to normal.

There isn't a perfect or simple answer. In Chapter 2, you will read about how the complex challenges of closing during the pandemic are distinct from reopening. However, recognizing that the problem is complex is the first step to adopting a new mindset for better decision-making.

May 27, 2020: Still a Target, Still a Leader

In the core of my 2016 letter "Company Talk about Police Shootings, as Target and CEO" I acknowledged my own painful emotions after the killings of Philando Castile and Alton Stewart.[28] I hoped to create space for our employees, to feel theirs. In the two days after May 25, 2020, I felt the same emotional, exhausted haze from the footage of the murder of George Floyd. It was a reminder: I'm *still* a target, and I'm *still* a leader. I wrote this in my blog:

> We are a different company now, five times larger across 20 states, maintaining ~55% she/her pronouns,

35% BIPOC, and 23% LGBTQIA+ folks among the 125 professional staff. We've navigated the challenges of scaling a distributed company, while staying connected through crises like #metoo, detention centers, and now COVID. I remain impressed that most of our fundamental distributed connection practices were conceived, designed, and executed by Trussels, whether individually or in affinity groups and facilitation guilds.

Despite this, I've learned how hard it is for employees to claim time to be human, especially in the last few months. We've been programmed with so many powerful messages that "good employees are quiet employees," that it takes repeated, insistent invitation before people will admit the emotional turmoil and burnout underneath. Only then will they respond to the nudge to take a 5-minute meditation, a 20-minute walk, a 50-minute virtual therapy, or an 8-hour PTO [paid time off] day.

There's a lot of overdue talk about "taking care of your people," sparked by how to keep employees connected during the pandemic. The idea that we are *human* seems to be intruding into our work consciousness. There's greater awareness and access to mental health resources as well as the recognition that psychological safety is a fundamental premise for great performance. The leaders I admire are addressing the new reality with new tools, whether it's communicating a layoff or helping people adjust to working from home. It's hard, emotional, necessary work for leaders.

And then there are days when it's harder.

Proposal: Adopt a New Mindset for Making Decisions

Consider the following perspective: At the start of the 2020s, we have been presented with a worldwide experiment that affects everything from education to health policy. We have a global control condition – what happens when you shut down offices and confine people to homes? Academic and leadership careers will be made because these conditions reveal some basic assumptions that we could never explore in depth before. For example, most of our beliefs about work and productivity *assume a building*, whether it is an office, store, or factory. Many of our so-called best practices *assume face-to-face interaction*. How many of our theories of innovation *assume in-person serendipity* like the proverbial water cooler conversation? Challenging these assumptions opens up multitudes of options to observe, experiment, and rethink. But if being confronted with the evidence that our offices were not founts of creative innovation, but of status-enforcing, energy-sapping activity without meaningful output, leaders may not make the best decisions for themselves or their companies.

Instead, imagine a different mindset. John DeGioia, Chancellor of Georgetown University, was hired with a "simple" task – create the twenty-first-century university.[29] Sounds exciting, except there was the constraint that this modern university must respect over 200 years of academic history and 2000 years of Jesuit / Christian history. In other words, his mandate was actually a complex problem – is there a singular answer to "What is a twenty-first-century university?" He believed there were changes needed that they could not predict in advance, and thus not plan for in a traditional way. Instead, he encouraged his team and department heads to collaborate, experiment, and iterate. He knew this would be a challenge for professors and department chairs, and he needed to create room for them to fail – not the usual mandate for proud academic departments.

In a speech where he described the project, Chancellor DiGioia reflected that he told his teams: "We have a result that's not what we expected, and we will have to do something different . . . will you follow me anyway?" We've been trained to assume systems are complicated when they are complex. We often have reflexive reactions to stress, and as a result, we can make poor decisions. In particular, the simple, but profound decision to take a public stand on a controversial issue can render the most experienced leaders silent with fear of making a mistake. However, my proposal is that we can practice methods to explore uncertainty and complexity with curiosity, create processes to enable others to follow, and train ourselves to sustain our efforts without burning out. Move to the Edge, Declare It Center doesn't protect you from making mistakes. It doesn't ensure that you will always have the best answer. What I hope you get out of this book is that intentional practice, both exterior with our teams and organizations, and interior with ourselves, will enable you to make better decisions.

Part 1

WHAT IS MOVE TO THE EDGE, DECLARE IT CENTER?

Making decisions under complexity and uncertainty requires *sustained* effort. The framework is composed of the methods of *Move to the Edge* and processes of *Declare It Center*. This combination enables others to participate, iterate scale, and sustain throughout the team or organization.

The methods of Move to the Edge and the processes of Declare It Center are both composed of a series of practices, Exterior and Interior. The Exterior Practices are visible, consisting of documents, playbooks, and processes. The Interior Practices are emotional, consisting of habits, inner work, and behaviors. Both are crucial. Exterior Practices alone can create the illusion of omniscience, ill-prepared for the impact of human feelings. Interior Practices alone don't enable others to follow, share, and improve one's own work. Both are needed for organizations to move through complex, uncertain situations, and to then center on systems to sustain, scale, and share the work.

Chapter 1

A FRAMEWORK TO MAKE DECISIONS UNDER COMPLEXITY AND UNCERTAINTY

I have a long history with insomnia. I wake up around 2 a.m. and stay awake for several hours. In Brazil, this time is called the *madrugada*, a time for creative expression without the filter of rational, conscious thinking.[1] At my best, I use the time to pursue my curiosity, making connections between different domains in art, sports, psychology, and history. Like the phenomenon of getting your best ideas in the shower, I dictate ideas into my phone without censoring. Most ideas are worthless, but I value the exploration.

One night in 2015, I was watching *Andy Warhol, A Documentary Film*[2] on the career of Andy Warhol. My curiosity was piqued because both my parents share his hometown of Pittsburgh, Pennsylvania, and my great-uncle Mozelle, another gay, Pittsburgh-native visual artist, arrived in New York during the same period in the early 1960s.

The New York art scene in the late 1950s and early 1960s was dominated by the abstract expressionists – Jackson Pollock and Willem De Kooning, for example – and the galleries and patrons were uninterested in Andy Warhol. His style couldn't be more antithetical to the intuitive sweeps and drops of Jackson Pollock, and he couldn't get anyone to show his Campbell's Soup can paintings. His first show was in Los Angeles, and with that success, Warhol doubled down on his art, started The Factory in 1962, and proceeded to upend the art establishment.[3] He had a vivid impact on culture for the next two decades.

So how did Warhol overturn the dominance of the Expressionist crowd into the era-defining movement of "pop art"? According to art historian Dave Hickey, Warhol declared, "This is the new world of art we need to live in; the rest is history." The established art world had to address his work, even if only by dismissing and denigrating it. As a result, Warhol turned the conversation onto himself on his terms, garnering more attention, and gaining more acolytes in fellow artists and buyers. It was a brilliant strategy, summarized by Hickey in this quote:

Move to the edge, declare it the center, and let the world reorganize itself around you.

I immediately stopped the video and replayed that section to make sure I heard it right. I did a voice recording of the backstory, and as I did, I felt my cheeks radiating heat in the *madrugada* winter darkness.

THIS. This was the core of what we were doing at Truss. We were building a values-driven, remote-first, diverse software company. I was a Black non-engineering CEO with two technical cofounders, and we were digging into our own pockets without the help of investors. As my cofounder Mark said, "We run *to* the trash fires instead of away from them," because we wanted to tackle the most complex, challenging, and impactful problems.

It took almost a decade since the founding of Truss for the world to reorganize itself, but now our decisions to be remote-first and highly diverse look a lot more prescient.

Why? Because the nature of systems and problems has changed from complicated to complex, how we approach our work has newfound currency.

What Is Move to the Edge?

Move to the Edge is about being on the boundary of your knowledge and the unknown. Move to the Edge involves methods for discovering insights by creating experiments, iterating quickly, and identifying levers of change. It involves intersecting with other boundaries and overlapping with other people's mental models, networks, or schools of thought. It can open up different perspectives and insights that cannot be viewed from the center. Most importantly, Move to the Edge starts with a verb. *Move* is a series of actions fueled by intent, desire, and curiosity.

Even if we are highly accomplished, we can always move to the edge of our knowledge. There are many examples of elite athletes, musicians, and artists practicing skills on the edge of their ability, more than skills at the center of their craft. That's Michael Jordan developing a late-career turnaround jump shot. That's John Coltrane and Sonny Rollins taking a year off from performing and recording to develop the sound that influenced the next generation of jazz saxophonists. Indeed, Move to the Edge is one of the core principles of mastery.

You might conclude that moving to the edge is purely by choice. There's one problem: When the context shifts, you might find yourself *moved* to the edge. Ask Kodak, Blockbuster, and BlackBerry about being oblivious, slow, or resistant to consumer shifts. Instead of being the center, we can find ourselves at the edge, and suddenly many of our assumptions must be questioned.

When the pandemic hit, people around the world found themselves working from home. Think about all the assumptions about what the center was in January 2020, for everyone. These assumptions are no longer valid because it is starkly clear that there will be a new normal in the 2020s.

The process of Move to the Edge is *most* important when the context suddenly changes. When I spoke on a panel on Business Transformation in September 2020 with leaders from Accenture, The Gap, and Salesforce, I learned that the pandemic sparked more investment in digital transformation in 3 months than in the prior 10 years. The methods of Move to the Edge are preparation for these shifts, so that leaders can make the right investments, aimed at the right outcomes, for the right purpose.

As I've developed this framework, I've noticed that the edge also carries an emotional response. For some, the edge is scary and dangerous, a misstep away from falling off a cliff – and thus should be avoided. For others, it's a thrilling, dopamine-generating experience that is clarifying and addicting. The edge can have all of those connotations, but the core is that the boundary of one's knowledge, experience, and practice is the edge. Because the edge is both a cognitive and emotional experience, the Move to the Edge, Declare It Center framework has practices – Exterior and Interior – that address both.

What Is Declare It Center?

The process of Declare It Center is about taking new information and insights and building operations to systematize, scale, and share these innovations so that they deliver the desired outcome. The infrastructure that supports Declare It Center enables individuals, teams, and companies to sustain their work with less individual effort.

One of my favorite examples of infrastructure is the process for painting the Golden Gate Bridge. The schedule for painting the bridge starts with the same section on the same day each year. They progress from one section to another until they reach the end of the bridge, and then they begin again on the first section one year later on the same date. This system is easy to follow, is predictable, and achieves the outcome of having a freshly painted landmark without recalculating the schedule each year.

I became interested in infrastructure after Truss helped fix Healthcare.gov. I began to recognize that our approach to solving complex problems seemed to have a pattern. As I mentioned in the introduction, *agile development* describes an iterative, customer-centric pattern of building that Truss uses successfully with our clients. However, agile development doesn't describe the full story of its impact on people who aren't directly building software. I became curious if there were concepts or theories that captured some of the social psychology of this dynamic, because as many leaders will attest, the hardest part of change is not the software – it's the people.

In 2015, I discovered a concept called *infrastructuralism*. Infrastructuralism is based on the observation that there is a dynamic relationship between software, architecture, and the experience that humans want from that software. This fit the pattern we observed at Truss. Designing an infrastructure that coordinates people, technology, and operations is a key part of Declare It Center. It is a better match to the challenge posed by complex problems because it assumes there are unknowns, and it creates a space to engage multiple perspectives in order to make higher-quality decisions.

While infrastructuralism was an important construct, it didn't inspire action. In short, it wasn't a verb. That evening, watching a documentary about Andy Warhol, I learned the verbs to describe our practice at Truss. Now it's time to share that practice with you.

Chapter 2

EXTERIOR PRACTICES: THE METHODS OF MOVE TO THE EDGE

The word *edge* connotes multiple, powerful meanings. It's the sharp end of a blade, an incisive quality, or the hint of discomfort with a person or experience. It's also a position furthest away from the center, an intersection of two boundaries, or the moment before "shit goes down." I've noticed that *edge* also carries an emotional response. For some, the edge is scary and dangerous, a misstep away from falling off a cliff. For others, it's a thrilling, dopamine-generating experience that can be clarifying and addicting. *Edge* can have all of those connotations, but the essence is that the boundary of knowledge, experience, and practice carries uncertainty. When "I don't know," "I have no idea," or "I don't think I can do this," flashes across your brain, welcome to your edge. The challenge is not to react to the thrill or the danger, but to develop the skill to be *still*.

Being still creates the opportunity to open new vantage points. You stay long enough to intersect and exchange at the boundary of other people's experiences. You start to see different perspectives up close that are obscured from your center. Being still with the uncertainty long enough has a payoff – you make a conscious decision, not a reaction to the feeling itself. Ultimately, Move to the Edge is a verb – a series of actions fueled by intent, desire, and curiosity.

Even if we are very accomplished, we can always Move to the Edge. In fact, managing the uncertainty on the edge is a skill that elite athletes, musicians, and artists practice. Psychologist Anders Ericsson showed that masterful people practice on the edge of their ability, not those at the center of their craft.[1] Simone Biles developed moves that no one else could perform *after* she was a two-time Olympic gold medalist. Many of the guests in one of my favorite podcasts, *Finding Mastery* by sports psychologist Michael Gervais, explicitly talk about practicing at the edge, including the downsides and sacrifices that come with it.

The global COVID pandemic should end any doubt that no one is immune from finding themselves at the edge through no action of their own. Like many new skills, we're probably not very good at being still with uncertainty yet. Instead, with practice, we can start responding with curiosity instead of anxiety, which opens our eyes to seeing from a new vantage point.

This impact of the pandemic was felt in cities around the world, but to illustrate, consider the daily experience of San Francisco Bay residents in November 2019. Lucky ones were excited to be new Golden State Warriors season ticket holders, others were planning long indoor brunches or late-night clubbing, planning Burning Man camps, or preparing for second semesters. Growing companies were drawing up open office plans in expensive downtown San Francisco real estate. Meanwhile, their workers were trying to afford ever-increasing monthly rentals by tripling occupancies or trying out "dorm hotels." Retail and manufacturing businesses were expecting cargo ship deliveries from Shanghai, China, to the Port of Oakland, California, and looking forward to earning back their investments in spring and summer shopping.

By June 2020, consider these choices from a new vantage point. What is the trade-off of expensive leased office space, long commutes, and prohibitive residential rent prices versus working from home, across multiple locations, and investing in good communication systems? What is the risk of not having multiple sources of rare metals or alternative production locations versus the cost of investing in new software infrastructure and modernized data pipelines for better forecasting?

The practices in Move to the Edge don't protect you from making mistakes. They don't ensure that you always have the right answer – if it's a complex problem, it's unlikely there is one! What Move to the Edge will do is enable you to approach the problem and make better decisions. It will show you the value of saying, "I don't know." It will show you how to be still with uncertainty.

The methods of Move to the Edge have Exterior practices that can be used with teams and companies. The most frequently used Exterior practices will be shown in this chapter, then you'll read about them in action in Part Two. The book is not intended to be a comprehensive list, however. Teams and companies develop new practices all the time, which makes this emerging perspective exciting. What unites these practices is a bias toward an experimental mindset, a curiosity to learn, the willingness to be wrong, and the rigor to test, repeat, and scale.

More inquiry, less certainty.[2]

There's a lot of wisdom in starting with questions. But, like many leaders trained in traditional education and management systems, I've been rewarded most of my life for having "the answer" – whether I'm right is another matter. In complex systems, the skill to master is asking better questions. I can shift my perspective to a new vantage point, or even better, create space for others to inquire from their own perspective.

In the next section, I detail some of the Move to the Edge methods we use at Truss, both internally and with our clients.

Forming Hypotheses

While not as formal as a scientific or academic hypothesis, developing a testable hypothesis in business is critical for taking a hunch and turning it into a concrete project. A good hypothesis document describes the problem, obstacle, and/or opportunity to be addressed. It details the outcome if the hypothesis is true, and the method for testing the hypothesis. At Truss, we have bias toward action, so we adjust how rigorous the hypothesis needs to be according to the risk and consequences of the decision. If a course of action is reversible and low impact, a less formal hypothesis is sufficient. Finally, the most important thing is to learn, not to be correct. When we set this standard, then it is easier to spread an experimental mindset throughout the organization because there is less fear of a failed hypothesis.

- **Brainstorming.** At Truss, we don't do typical brainstorming, where people go around the table giving their ideas. There's a lot of research that this format tends to reinforce the loudest voices, and dampen dissenting perspectives, which can result in poor decisions.[3] Instead, we ask people to write down their responses individually, in silence, and then submit them to the group. This especially engages more introverted people, as well as people who process written information more slowly. Depending on the situation, we make the responses anonymous so that people at all levels might take the risk to write a distinct or dissenting viewpoint. We find that giving questions in advance often results in more thoughtful, reflective, and creative responses.

- **"How might we . . ." and other open-ended questions.** Shifting to open-ended questions is a simple but powerful technique to elicit more creative, edge-pushing thinking. Our design and research practices use these questions in user, client, and operator research, and we use these internally in our own hypothesis sessions. Bonus – make sure to ask yourself who is the "we" answering that question. If "we" represents only one point of view, skill set, hierarchy, race or gender, the next action is to redefine the "we" to include diverse perspectives.

- **Beliefs, Facts, Data.** This is a simple but effective way to generate hypotheses, especially when there are strongly held, opposing points of view. Make a chart with columns headed with Beliefs, Facts, and Data, and rows headed by Opinion. An individual or a group fills in each of the cells. What typically happens is that there are many beliefs that don't have facts or data, or people list the same fact but draw different beliefs from them. The value of this chart is that information becomes actionable. If there is a lack of data for a belief, the team can design hypotheses and a test to generate that data, and confirm or refute the belief.

Hypothesis Testing

There are many different ways to gather data, quantitative or qualitative, in order to validate a hypothesis. A few that we most commonly use are listed below:

- **Surveys.** The notion of a survey is straightforward, but there is a science to constructing good questions, ordering those questions, survey length, and survey setting that is beyond the scope of this book. That said, we are mindful that we are renting someone's time, so we have a bias toward short, infrequent surveys, and we take pains to make sure the survey taker feels their time is being used wisely. It may be difficult to design the perfect survey, but it is possible to identify the limitations of the survey, and draw directionally correct, if modest conclusions from it.

- **User research.** Similar to surveys, there are many techniques for conducting user research, and cataloguing them all would be beyond the scope of this book. However, the critical takeaway for the reader is that *listening* to real people, *empathizing* with their challenges, and *observing* them in their context are skills that can be learned by anyone. These often generate unique insights and, in my experience, are underutilized by organizations. These interviews can be overdone, however, and there are methods to conduct the right amount of interviews to validate a hypothesis.[4]

- **Customer development.** Popularized by Steve Blank in *The Four Steps to the Epiphany: Successful Strategies for Products that Win*,[5] and Eric Ries in *The Lean Startup*,[6] customer development emphasized "getting out of the office" to learn from customers directly about their problems in the context of their experience. Those stories inform hypotheses about customer needs which can be validated in iterative experiences with customers, until the key elements of a successful product or service is clear. In this process, it is just as important to *invalidate* a hypothesis. A great resource for constructing great invalidating questions is Cindy Alvarez's *Customer Development*.[7]

- Learning that your product doesn't solve a customer problem early prevents the mistake of spending millions to develop a product that your customer doesn't want.

    I've experienced this personally. Early in the development of our mobile app, Leave Now, I insisted on spending $5,000 (a large sum for bootstrapping founders with no income) on a specific design and font, because I believed we had to make our interface distinctive and appealing. I didn't ask any of our core customers (executive assistants) for feedback or confirm whether these designs would make a difference. Not only did the designs make no appreciable difference, but they were "hardcoded," which meant that changing and maintaining them cost more than the designs themselves.

Eventually, we reverted to standard fonts and design elements, and I learned a valuable, if embarrassing, lesson.

• **Discovery and framing.** One of the practices we've used at Truss is discovery and framing. Essentially, it is a technique to open the aperture of our client's thinking about a particular problem. Many of our clients, with the benefit of history and expertise, are convinced they fully understand the problem – and they're not wrong. However, after we ask their customers, partners, and even their own employees, client leaders recognize they don't have the complete picture, and we can start developing more informed approaches to solving a problem.

Iteration and Fast Feedback

We use iteration and fast feedback so much at Truss that I almost forgot to include this as one of our practices for this book. We draft presentations, build software, and test policies with an assumption that it will go through cycles of iteration. At core is the belief that input, testing, and feedback will make it better. This approach is common in other domains, from K–12 educational assessment to using limited movie releases to learn how audiences will respond.

There are a few important steps to make this successful. First, do it early, to expose core assumptions at play that might need revision. Second, ask people for candid, concrete feedback, by telling them what your objectives are, why their perspectives matter, and how you will consider them. Finally, put it on repeat. Frequent, fast iterations create concrete links between feedback and response. By telling your customers, partners, or employees that you will be iterating at a planned cadence – we recommend between one and two weeks – you build trust and momentum.

Project Scoping

Scoping at Truss is similar to getting an estimate from an architect before hiring a contractor to remodel your kitchen. You want to learn that your vision for a dream kitchen carries a risk of collapsing your roof because it will remove a load-bearing wall. Project scoping identifies constraints, risks, and opportunities to mitigate those risks. At its best, project scoping is a good example of bringing together multiple points of view to reduce the likelihood of blind spots and unknowns.

We perform a rigorous discovery in order to identify different types of risk, including technology, execution, resource, competitive, and financial. We audit operations, technology, and customers, but we also engage employees delivering the technology. Accounting for context, relationships – and yes, emotions – is part of our toolkit for identifying risk. At the close of scoping, the combination of a plan and an iterative process create the platform for identifying "that which is fragile" and solving that FIRST.

Project scoping is especially important in environments like government, health care, and financial systems, where concerns of compliance, privacy, and security are a high priority. A few of our principles include:

- Hire high-caliber talent with a strong filter for collaboration and communication.

- Utilize adaptive processes, like iterative development, and attack the riskiest issues first.

- Make those choices trivially transparent, so the work of solving the problem is simultaneously the communication signal that the problem is being worked on.

- Use short-time-span reviews, like retrospectives, to assess progress on problems and recalibrate if necessary.

Scoping is a key system approach at Truss. This is a Move to the Edge method to identify risk and unknowns, and to uncover assumptions. Scoping can be used for any type of project, large or small, for external clients or for your own organizations. In the Salary Transparency case study, you will see how we used project scoping to change our internal policies and practices.

Who Is in the Room Where It Happens? Bringing in Diverse Voices

When I was a young associate consultant at Bain and Company, I got sage advice from an experienced African American senior consultant. "Always be nice to the receptionist at the client's office. They know *everything*." I nodded but I didn't need to be told. My mother was a receptionist at IBM in the late 1960s in New York's Hudson Valley. Not only did she know a lot, but also she noticed how the customers were changing from universities and military agencies toward large corporations and manufacturers. This observation inspired her to become one of the first Black female programmers, right at the transition between mainframe computers to early laptop computers.[8] Paying attention is a skill set of many frontline workers, and when complex problems need more diverse insights, it is smart to design systems that allow for their input.

At Truss, we will talk directly to customers, end users, and operators of systems not only at the beginning of discovery and framing, but through the design and building of a system. As a result, not only we will we learn needs, problems, desires, and frustrations, we will build trust and increase the probability of success – and the probability of being invited back.

You might choose to focus on the operators of your systems, from customer service reps, to executive assistants, dispatchers, or system administrators. They are a treasure trove of data for how to design and build systems correctly. This diversity of experience, expertise, background, and vantage point is crucial to developing insights that make the difference between a great decision and one that has catastrophic consequences.

Example: Race and Artificial Intelligence

I arrive at Salt Lake City airport after a three-hour flight from the East Coast. Needing a refresh, I turn into the bathroom, crowded with fellow travelers. When I get to the bank of sinks, I put my hand under the automated soap dispenser. Nothing happens. I circle my hand clockwise, I circle my hand counterclockwise. I move my hand closer, then farther, and my pantomime becomes even more apparent as I notice all the people to my left and right soaping, washing, and drying without thinking. I look up at myself in the mirror, annoyed and self-conscious because I'm the only one. The only Black person at the sinks, and the only one – again – wondering how many tries before the sensor sees my hand.

If you are a person with dark skin, I suspect you knew the punch line of the story within the first three sentences. You know because this experience is so common that it deserves a mini-celebration when the soap comes out the first time. Being unseen is nothing new, so it is no surprise that sensors are not designed for you.

If you are a light, white, or Caucasian person, I suspect that story might be a surprise. You've never heard of this, you've never noticed, and it didn't happen to you. For others, you are probably already doing an internet search to verify the story, either out of curiosity or skepticism. I'll save you the work – many ordinary sensors, from soap dispensers, sleep rings, to photography equipment were not designed to see dark skin.[9]

But let me expand the frame.

Imagine you are on the product team that is approving the sensors and the algorithms that will become de facto standard for autonomous trucks around the world. These sensors enable the trucks to drive themselves, avoiding collisions with other vehicles and stopping to protect the lives of pedestrians, from inattentive walkers to kids chasing a soccer ball that bounced into the street.

Now that you've heard my soap sensor story, does it change the questions you would ask in your product meeting? Would you look around the room at your teammates and wonder, are we missing someone? Does it make you consider what other facets of the problem you are not seeing?

In an airport bathroom, the soap sensors that don't see me are an annoyance. But there is no amount of handwaving that will prevent a 40-ton autonomous tractor–trailer from killing me in the crosswalk on a Tuesday evening when you've designed a sensor that can't see me. If you imagine your sensor design could become the standard in Jakarta, Nairobi, Bogota, or Houston, how does that feel in your body in this moment?

If you're a melanated person, and you're on that product team, you know what the stakes are. The questions are different. How do you speak up? Do you look around the room, calculating whether you'll get shut down or backed up? Even when you speak, will you be listened to with curiosity or disdain? This is a daily experience for many people who have darker skin, and it is a daily experience in that we are creating algorithms that are not designed for everybody on the planet – and some of these algorithms are fatal.

This story illustrates why the practices, methods, and mindsets of *Move to the Edge, Declare It Center* are critical for addressing complex problems. How do you incorporate the diverse perspectives to ensure that your decisions don't unwittingly kill thousands of people around the world? This is a reason to create diverse teams, and to create an inclusive environment to explore, inquire, challenge, and learn. This is why you develop systems that don't rely on your individual initiative or brilliance.

Whether engaging diverse voices is called accessibility, inclusiveness, human-centered, or talk story, your work will be better.[10] But we have to learn to assume the unknown, that you *don't* know, and then seek others who can help you discover so that everybody can benefit. It's a simple, powerful change, but it requires effort and intent to turn it into practice and habit. Whether your focus is livable cities, homelessness policy, power grids, climate change, health care, racial injustice, or forest fires, *this* is the job of the twenty-first-century leader.

Case Study: How We Made Salaries Transparent

In the Introduction, I introduced *why* we made salaries transparent at my company, Truss. Now that you've read about complex problems and the methods of Move to the Edge, we can dive deep into *how* we made salaries transparent.

Our first act was to admit that we didn't know how. We started with a question. How can we create a method about how to proceed? As I mentioned in Project Scoping, we started with the issue that was most fragile. Will people leave? So we surveyed employees immediately, and 19 out of 20 people gave a thumbs-up to moving forward. The 20th had concerns, but wanted to keep exploring as well. No one wanted to leave. Success!

The second question to consider was: Is this the right problem? We researched about salary disparities, root causes, and different methods for addressing it. We looked to companies like Buffer, who made salaries transparent earlier and posted their own process in public forums. Notably, we invalidated the hypothesis that the gender disparity is because "men negotiate their salaries, but women do not." In fact, the data show that even when women negotiate their salaries, they are systematically paid less than male counterparts for the same job.[11]

The third question was: Will people trust us? It was crucial to get this right. One of the aspects of Move to the Edge that I consistently get wrong is that I underestimate how much communication and repetition is required to bring people along the journey that involves change. Luckily, my cofounder Jen is a stickler for good communication plans, while Mark, my other cofounder, is a stickler for showing our work to keep people up to date and setting expectations for when things will be delivered.

Next question: Are our salary levels and performance bands correct? Oops, we realized this was a piece of infrastructure that was missing because we didn't have enough rigor in our bands. We did our research on banding and constructed a new performance rubric. Crucially, we included people at different levels of the organization to help, comment, and give feedback. This was by far the heaviest effort of the entire project.

Jen Leech describes more about leveling:

A leveling matrix is a rubric for establishing the skill level of an employee in their discipline. We wanted to be very clear about what we were measuring. What constitutes success in this role for Truss may not necessarily be the same for someone generic in the industry. Before we created a leveling system, we were using something called the Dreyfus model of skills acquisition, which is a five-level model of mastery. We would assign people a level within that, then we would use it as the reference point from the market to assign salaries.

Once we established our bands, the next question to ask was: Are we over- or underpaying anyone? Once we got industry data, we could compare our own compensation levels to industry standards.

The clearest cases to resolve were those in which we discovered we were underpaying a person relative to their level. In those cases, we could make the appropriate increases. More challenging was recognizing when we were overpaying an employee. Fortunately, this was rare. In those cases, we made the decision to keep the employee at their current salary level. Ultimately, responsibility for proper leveling rested on me and the other founders, so we committed never to reduce salary, because that mistake was ours. Both decisions demonstrated our commitment to the company that our goal was equity, but not at the expense of the employees.

Finally, what were the "unknown unknowns"? We conducted premortems, a method to project into the future in order to uncover risks (this is covered in Chapter 3) to make sure that we got different perspectives both inside and outside the company. Then we created transparent decision records to make sure that whoever succeeds us in managing the process could understand what we were doing and why.

Table 2.1 summarizes our questions and our practices.

Analyzed from a different perspective, the Move to the Edge methods function to systematically reduce the risk of a complex problem. We addressed the most important risk first (*the fragile*), then progressed through each new risk until we felt comfortable with the solution. From start to finish, this process lasted about 10 months until we were ready to announce it in our fourth-quarter stakeholder meeting with our employees.

TABLE 2.1   Move to the Edge Questions and Practices

Edge Question	Move to the Edge Practice
Will people leave?	Survey
Is this the right problem?	Discovery and training
Will people trust us?	Transparent communications, process, timeline
Are our levels and bands right?	Inclusive research
Are we over- or underpaying now?	Inclusive research
What are the unknown unknowns?	Premortem

Well . . . what happened?!

Ho-hum.

No fights. No resignations. Of course, people were curious, and I'm sure most employees checked the salary spreadsheet that day. Other than that, people returned to doing great work. Except one. A week later, an employee told us that another employee, based on the salary guidelines, needed to be paid more. After looking at the data, we realized not only was she correct, but we overlooked including a communication path to escalate anomalies like this.

Building systems to ensure that a solution to a complex problem can be repeated is a signal to begin a process of Declare It Center. We needed to build an infrastructure system through which we could scale, share, and sustain the work of making salaries transparent. If we were successful, salary transparency would become an ordinary part of our normal operations. We'll return to Salary Transparency in a case study in Chapter 3, "Exterior Practices: The Process of Declare It Center."

The patterns of navigating through uncertainty and unknowns aren't isolated to Truss, a software company, or even an organization. In the next case, I'll share a historic example, where the methods of Move to the Edge made a profound impact on our conception of a thriving, livable city.

Case Study: Jane Jacobs: What Kind of Problem Is a City?

"We have to understand cities as complex organisms, as problems of organized complexity."

—Jane Jacobs

Imagine 1950s postwar New York – flexing itself as the world's greatest city in the world's greatest country. New York's primary flexor was Robert Moses, the powerful public official who shaped mid-century urban development, not just for New York City, but for many cities across the United States. His vision was that the key to the modern city was the automobile, the highway, and the suburbs – not public transit, pedestrian life, and heterogeneous neighborhoods.

From the early 1930s through the early 1960s, he engineered the creation of bridges such as the Triborough, Verrazzano, and Throgs Neck, among others, connecting and bisecting the five boroughs of New York. Taking advantage of federal funding for the new Interstate Highway system, he constructed the Cross-Bronx, the Brooklyn-Queens, and Staten Island Expressways. These were among the first interstates to go *through* a city in the United States, which helped usher in the development of the first postwar suburbs, such as Levittown, New York.

But what of the people living in the city? Influenced by Swiss–French urban theorist Le Corbusier, Moses viewed cities, highways, and buildings primarily from above, as if they were dioramas, well outside of human scale. As a result, humans were often an afterthought, best clustered in functional, unadorned, high-rise buildings, connected via highway to suburbs, instead of smaller single and multifamily homes served by public transit.[12]

In particular, he believed that residents of poor and working-class neighborhoods were a visible blight on the modern city. These neighborhoods lacked the political leverage that wealthier communities possessed, and they were targeted by Moses to be demolished in favor of his "modern" vision. He didn't interview or gather data about what residents needed, largely because he didn't care.[13] His personal belief was that "these people" needed to make way for "progress." The legacies of Robert Moses in these neighborhoods are the brutalist high-rises we now know as "The Projects" and the scar of "urban renewal" that destroyed Black, Chinese, Japanese, and Latino neighborhoods in New York, Chicago, Durham, Miami, San Francisco, and Oakland.

His capstone was going to be the Lower Manhattan Expressway that would cut Manhattan from the Hudson on the west to the East River, connecting New Jersey to the burgeoning suburbs on Long Island to the east (Figure 2.1). Conceived in the 1940s, Moses got approval in 1960 from the NYC Planning Commission to proceed with construction that would go right through Greenwich Village, parts of SoHo and Little Italy, destroy Washington Square Park, displace 800 businesses, and evict 2,000 families (Figure 2.2).[14]

Enter Jane Jacobs, an architecture journalist, neighborhood observer, and resident of Greenwich Village (Figure 2.3). Over the years of writing articles about different local neighborhoods in Manhattan, she noticed a set of patterns, and it prompted her to ask a very different set of questions than those asked by Robert Moses.

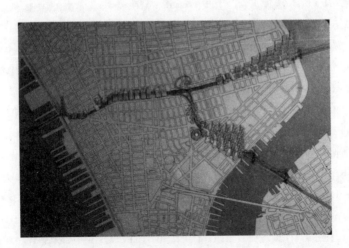

FIGURE 2.1   Planned route of the Lower Manhattan Expressway.
Courtesy: Library of Congress.

FIGURE 2.2 Washington Square Park, from the 9th floor of NYU's Kimmel Center, on the south side of the park.

Joe Mabel, CC BY-SA 3.0

What kind of problem are cities?

In *Death and Life of Great American Cities*, she writes, "Cities are problems of organized complexity."[15] She nailed the essence of the issue 60 years ago – on page 2! The rest of the book elaborates on her research and vision, but in 1960, she had a more pragmatic problem to solve: How can she stop a highway from destroying her neighborhood? Turns out, she started using some of the same methods from Move to the Edge.

She asked questions and made observations about what makes a neighborhood livable. She surveyed parents, garbagemen, shop owners, seamstresses, and other residents who had different but aligning lifestyles, and their intersecting needs were often satisfied by their neighborhoods. For Jacobs, it's *humans* that make cities livable. Narrow streets prevent large, fast-moving traffic from endangering pedestrians. Residents with windows

FIGURE 2.3   Jane Jacobs.

Phil Stanziola, Public domain, via Wikimedia Commons

facing the street can collectively serve to watch over their neighbors because they are in close proximity. Mixed-use neighborhoods with small shops, restaurants, and residents can create resilient, local ecosystems, which was a powerful economic lever that sustained segregated Black, Japanese, and Chinese neighborhoods in the United States. Unfortunately, many of these communities were destroyed by a combination of racism, urban renewal, and – in the case of the Greenwood neighborhood of Tulsa, Oklahoma – a mob of White vigilantes who set fire to the "Black Wall Street" in 1921.[16]

In other words, Jacobs's human-centered method was a radical departure from Moses's large-scale urban planning approach. In today's language, she was a *disruptor,* using the methods of survey, hypothesis testing, customer development with diverse parties to address a complex problem. From 1960 through 1964, Jacobs organized a coalition with a common goal: stop the Lower Manhattan Expressway.

But she was faced with a new question: How do we use the survey data, signatures, and testimony of neighborhood residents to influence city officials to make a better decision? They went to the "room where it happens" – public hearings. There was one problem. Robert Moses would employ the tactic to announce the time and location of public hearings without enough notice for residents to attend. The secrecy would ensure that the other city officials could follow his wishes without scrutiny from the press or the scorn of local residents.

But because Jacobs had developed allies, including political insiders who resented Moses's overbearing ambition, she got tipped off to times and locations, and brought her neighborhood with her. The combination of first-hand testimony and newly favorable press coverage for Jacobs's coalition changed the political calculus for city officials. In 1964, they rejected Moses's expressway. As you can imagine, Moses was not going to let a "housewife" beat him, so he doubled down and tried again with the Mid-Manhattan Expressway.[17]

Over those years of skirmishes, Jane Jacobs realized that the lynchpin to stopping urban redevelopment projects was not data or demonstrations. The key was preventing the designation *condemned*. Once a building was stamped as condemned by public officials, it was extremely difficult to prevent the city from razing it, clearing the space, and making the area uninhabitable. Stop the condemned designations and they could stop or delay neighborhoods from being destroyed. This was an unexpected solution to a complex problem, and from then on, she focused her tactics to achieve that objective. Combined with effective organizing, coalition-building, and first-hand data from neighborhoods, they defeated the Mid-Manhattan Expressway – and Robert Moses – once again.

Following these successes, they continued to hone their tactics, messaging, and campaigning to enable even more people to follow, successfully shifting public opinion against neighborhood-destroying development. Over the next five years, Jacobs and her coalition continued to focus on preserving the unique, human-scaled character of Manhattan's neighborhoods. Meanwhile, Robert Moses's power was greatly diminished through the rest of the 1960s, and his vision for highways and bridges crisscrossing New York City was effectively over.

Neither Moses nor Jacobs could have anticipated trends like the resurgence of vibrant urban centers, the decline of auto purchases by millennials, or ride-sharing services like Lyft succeeding taxis 50 years later. However, Jacobs's summation of a city as *organized complexity*, rooted in first-hand, human-centered data gathering, has proved to be highly influential for how we create livable, sustainable cities. Theory aside, she used Move to the Edge methods to question, test, build diverse coalitions, and ultimately persuade others to follow.

As a leader, you have an opportunity to follow her path, whether it's in your industry, company, or community. Walk the block, get out of the building, talk to your customers, and develop your own hypotheses. Using Move to the Edge methods can create a new vantage point for leaders to address complex problems in different ways than the center.

If you are a person who grew up on the edge because of your race, gender, place of birth, or physical body, you probably already realize the value of having a distinct vantage point. You witness policy decisions, and from the vantage point of being on the edge, recognize, "Hey, this policy is not designed with me in mind. This doesn't work for a lot of other people, as well." You can use the methods of Move to the Edge to test your hypothesis and challenge these decisions. In contrast, if you grew up in the center, you can still cultivate new vantage points by centering others who are different from you. Exterior practices like surveying diverse people are incredibly powerful ways to build allies and coalitions, highlight blind spots, and ultimately design a better solution.

If you build a Move to the Edge practice focused on discovering, experimenting, and iterating, then, as we'll see in Chapter 3, building Declare it Center processes to systematize, scale, share, and sustain your innovations can have lasting influence. Jane Jacobs and her coalition changed the course of New York City. Now let's look at a current example of using Move to the Edge methods to influence how we rebuild communities devastated by natural disasters and exacerbated by the COVID pandemic.

Case Study: World Central Kitchen

"You can't do this from an office, or from a command center headquarters somewhere. You have to get out and be boots on the ground."

Nate Mook, CEO World Central Kitchens

Chef José Andres founded World Central Kitchens (WCK) in 2010 to use the power of food to nourish communities and strengthen economies in times of crisis. They have developed a remarkable model of disaster response that adapts to local situations, resulting in delivering 50 million fresh meals to people around the world, from Haiti to Indonesia. Crises resulting from natural disasters are fraught with uncertainty, and I was curious whether they used Move to the Edge methods to navigate those intense situations.

Nate Mook, CEO of World Central Kitchens, described their approach. "There's the discovery component, which is so important because you're discovering two sides. The supply side is how we can produce what's needed – in this case, food and water. What are the resources and assets that are already there? Second, there is the demand side. What are the needs on the ground of the community?"

WCK starts with discovery, a key Move to the Edge method. By leading with inquiry, WCK is able to learn and adapt to the unique aspects of any situation. They don't do discovery at a distance. They contact people who are in the community itself. They fly to the areas affected by the disaster, and they talk directly with individuals, community leaders, government officials, food suppliers, and restaurant owners. The diversity of perspective is crucial not only to identifying the resources that are already there but to including the needs of the community *pre*-disaster in their assessment of the situation. This is diversity and inclusion in real-time, another Move to the Edge method.

He told a story of doing discovery after arriving in Lake Charles after Hurricane Laura devastated Louisiana in August 2020. "One of the first things we did was load up a Google maps satellite view. We look for the little white rectangular strips. Those are the trailer parks, which are some of the most vulnerable areas after a hurricane. Then we drive to the parks, walk around, knock on doors, and . . . talk to people. Are you okay? What's the damage? What do you need?" They are able to quickly get a direct, candid, vivid assessment of what's happening, but in a deceptively simple way. We both smiled as he continued, "This should not be innovative, but unfortunately, it is. Go to the places, talk to the people, and find out what the situation is like for them." It's a powerful set of Move to the Edge practices to navigating complexity.

As he was telling this story, it reminded me of Jane Jacobs developing her hypothesis to stop Robert Moses from destroying Lower Manhattan by walking the neighborhoods of Greenwich Village and Little Italy, talking to neighbors, store owners, and moms walking with their kids to the park. Both she and World Central Kitchens started with inquiry, did discovery, and developed hypotheses from the vantage point of the people closest to the situation. Both approaches are a contrast to the approach of Robert Moses in the early 1960s, and the typical approach of organizations like the Federal Emergency Management Agency (FEMA). Both Moses and FEMA make the mistake of thinking the system is complicated instead of complex, assessing the situation at a distance in a command center, and using a predetermined series of actions to get to the "right answer."

Historically, FEMA would observe a shortage of food and send millions of Meals Ready to Eat (MREs), or observe a shortage of bread in Puerto Rico and ship containers of bread to the island. But FEMA wouldn't ask people on the ground what they actually need. As a result, MREs sit on shelves uneaten, and bread goes stale. In contrast, by talking to people directly about what they need, WCK flips the question. How can we provide *nourishing* meals to communities after a disaster? How can we enable bakeries *to make bread* to nourish their neighbors?

By appreciating the complexity of the overlapping needs, from reviving economic livelihoods to restimulating local food production, WCK opens the aperture to creating novel solutions that also adapt to the specific local context.

But how can WCK do this across different types of disasters, different languages, customs, and environments? They Declare It Center, using processes, systems, and infrastructure to enable teams to follow and scale it so it can be applied across the world. I'll highlight how they do that in Chapter 3, "Exterior Practices: The Process of Declare It Center."

Case Study: Public Health Networks and the Early Days of COVID

One way I sought to test the hypothesis for Move to the Edge, Declare It Center outside of my company was to interview people with first-hand experience in complex situations. In particular, I wanted to speak to people where these situations were high intensity, high uncertainty, and coordinated decision-making has consequential outcomes. People in emergency response fit that profile. The opening to the 2020 decade was dominated by the COVID pandemic, and in the US and Australia, massive forest fires. I had the opportunity to learn from several people who played important front-line roles in responding to those crises. There is a history in studying their methods, processes, and infrastructure, but I wanted to learn first-hand from their moments of "I don't know."[18]

As a public health official, Daniella[19] had been through SARS, the Avian flu, Ebola, and H1N1, so when rumors of COVID in China first started coming out, she was familiar with novel viruses. However, four simultaneous trends signaled something different: shifting information out of China; evolving updates from the CDC to local public health officials; increasing numbers of "suspect" cases that needed to be assessed and tested; and finally, an overwhelming influx of questions and concerns from local clinicians and the public. Interpreting these trends, she started to activate her agency's emergency response infrastructure. "I remember the first time getting nervous when Italy's hospitals were overwhelmed, because that was another developed country," she recalled.

One thing that became clear is that public officials already had a tested response structure that they could adapt to most infectious diseases. Health departments that had been hit worst with HIV/AIDS, SARS, Ebola, or H1N1 had adapted their systems. So far, the pattern was familiar, even if the specifics were unknown.

"My story is that I have years of tight relationships with other public health leaders, epidemiologists and other infectious disease specialists. Many of us went through H1N1 and other public health emergencies together. At first, we would just ping each other and ask, "Are you seeing this in your area?" As the numbers increased and we started hearing the same thing from other parts of the country, we started to have weekly meetings, then increased to twice weekly, to check on how we were thinking about this problem." Across the country, the pattern of formal and informal networks of regional public health officials exchanging their experiences became more frequent in January and February 2020.

By March 1, when she declared a local public health emergency after the first case in her jurisdiction, many regional networks across the world realized that they had to act. First, large events were canceled, then smaller and smaller gatherings were also canceled until full shutdowns started. Finland was first, on March 8, followed by Italy on March 9, followed soon thereafter by most European countries. King County, WA, in the United States was the first to issue a limited shelter-in-place,[20] followed by a full shelter-in-place in the Bay Area on March 16 and the state of California three days later. Because COVID was global, those networks of data and information exchange were now on full tilt.

This is the importance of having diverse networks as part of Move to the Edge. These interconnected networks from different regions, states, countries, and continents were sharing data, practices, experiments, and results multiple times per day. Structures to report key data emerged, from CDC calls to the World Health Organization, to updates by regional networks. These evolved over time to reflect both growing knowledge and discarded hypotheses. It seemed chaotic at times as a layperson, but from the reports of people on the inside, these rapid iterations reflected a common, well-trained experimental mindset. Diverse networks with rapid iteration and scalable structures is a hallmark of great Move to the Edge, Declare It Center practices.

Most public health officials thought that the initial decision to shut things down would be the most difficult decision of their careers. However, the decisions about how to reopen things safely were much harder. "We didn't necessarily have evidence and data with this novel virus on how to best approach this. It's clear looking back to the influenza epidemic in 1918 which cities and countries shut down first and for how long. We knew those that shut down early and for longer actually had better recoveries, and it's easier to compare those actions with the eventual death toll," Daniella explained. "We incorporated that data about disease transmission into our models, but there's no literature that I know of that covers how cities reopened, which parts reopened first, and what the success of those decisions was," Daniella concluded.

Unlike the shelter-in-place, health officials were now in "I don't know" territory. They had to coordinate with many different stakeholders, from businesses to schools to transportation, in a political and civic context that is tricky at best, without great historical data or knowledge. The practice of iterating is challenging, too. Daniella reflected, "It's harder to say to a retail store owner or restaurant workers who have been hurting for months, 'We're going to test reopening for a week, evaluate, and then see what happens.' I don't know if it works well that way, because they can lose trust in us the next time we need to change a policy." As the Delta variant and other variants emerge, the question of closing and reopening will require more discovery and new hypotheses to rebuild that trust.

Chapter 3

EXTERIOR PRACTICES: THE PROCESS OF DECLARE IT CENTER

D eclare It Center is a set of processes to systematize, scale, share, and sustain the best approaches to solving complex problems and seizing new opportunities. It involves taking new information, discoveries, innovations, and data from Move to the Edge experiments, and then building infrastructure that embeds this new information into a repeatable, reliable system. Infrastructure is important because it coordinates people, technology, and operations, so that the new approach can scale, be shared, and be sustained. Without attention to Declare It Center processes, even the best solutions will fall short of the outcomes they were designed to achieve. This chapter will explore processes and case studies that different organizations and individuals use to Declare It Center. Before these case studies, let's look at a few short examples that expand on some of the concepts.

Like *edge*, the word *center* connotes a variety of meanings. A place of inner resolve, a sense of being "where it's at," a physical location, or the experience where everything revolves around you. For some, it feels like a destination to seek. For others, it's a place to launch from, alternating between edge and center. In my career as an entrepreneur, I have spent more time near or at the edge, where I collide with different people and ideas. But, my inherited center – born male, a United States citizen in the twentieth century – means that I will have the privilege and the blind spots that come from also being part of the center. For example, my board colleagues and the expert practitioners in the field at CARE consistently lift my head out of the US perspective, even as I'm conscious of lifting up the work of women and girls around the world.

At the core of Declaring It Center is creating ease. What starts as a heroic, brilliant, daring effort by an individual, team, or organization can wither into a discarded side project if they haven't built methods to create ease. An example of ease is the ability to find a "how-to" document written so a new person can follow. It's creating technical infrastructure to allow engineers to automate basic processes, freeing them to focus on more difficult problems. For leaders, it's building a shared sense of purpose by repeating, repeating, repeating core values and behaviors. These written, coded, and spoken processes are examples of Declare It Center infrastructure that create ease, allow people to follow, and enable the organization to turn a heroic effort into a sustainable program.

I'm particularly fond of finding examples of Declare It Center in nonprofits and social justice movements. When I remind people that the Montgomery Bus Boycott of 1955–1956 lasted 382 days, they are surprised. How did they sustain the effort to walk to work, through the heat of an Alabama summer? Rosa Parks and her compatriots were training at the Highlander Center in the Smoky Mountains of Tennessee for years *before* her famous refusal to move.[1] Community organizers had created plans and infrastructure, building relationships, to ensure that the Black workers would go along with the boycott and then built mutual aid and support systems so that the many months of walking to work, jail time, and threats could be withstood together.

Infrastructure is critical for nonprofits and social impact movements aiming to make systemic change. Systemic change requires *sustained* effort. Passion, righteous anger, and mass demonstration can spark an incredible outpouring of awareness and action. However, without building an infrastructure to sustain the effort, leaders and organizers often experience burnout. Precisely when their genius, insight, and novel solutions are needed most, their leaders' energy is depleted. From my experience on the board of CARE, Advisory Board of CASE, and as an employee at the Self-Help Credit Union, organizations that built infrastructure to sustain their innovations had a much better chance of surviving long enough to impact the systems they were seeking to change.

Building infrastructure, a critical component of Declare It Center, is not trivial or free. It takes expertise and experience to build systems to share information, measure impact, and manage customers. Building infrastructure is critical to delivering outcomes, but unfortunately, chronic underinvestment and disinterest by the funding community can hinder the systemic change they ultimately are seeking.

While I've highlighted examples from nonprofits and social change organizations in this introduction, the rest of Chapter 3 includes examples and case studies of how Declare It Center processes enabled organizations in different domains to sustain innovations and unique solutions to complex problems. The first example will be how Truss solved the complex problem of coordinating work in multiple locations, and then built Declare It Center infrastructure over the last decade to become a remote-first company that stretches across 30 states.

Building a Remote-First Company Before the Pandemic

In 2020 and 2021, the COVID pandemic and the Delta variant created tough choices about remote work for most leaders around the world. Even worse, these decisions were urgent, but many leaders lacked the experience or knowledge about how to enable their employees to work from home. We shared that urgency at Truss, but these decisions were a little easier, because we had almost a decade of working as a distributed, remote-first company.

I appreciate everyone who continues to confront the complex reality of remote and hybrid work. You have made courageous decisions, often without the benefit of experience or practice. As we know now, responding to COVID requires more than a temporary solution, so this section will give you pragmatic examples of the systems we developed at Truss to create a sustainable remote-first company. At the same time, this section will demonstrate specific Declare It Center processes to systematize, scale, share, and sustain the practices and innovations we made. I've included some of our most important structures to help you redesign any of your systems and practices.

First, a little history. My cofounders and I didn't initially envision Truss as a fully remote company. The decision was prompted by unforeseen circumstances when the company was founded in 2012. Mark Ferlatte and I recruited our third co-founder, Jennifer Leech, as we were launching Truss's first product, but there was one catch. Jen had to be out of the country for 18 months, traveling across numerous European countries. If we wanted to work together, we had to overcome the barrier of time and distance.

Fortunately, we had some experience already because in the mid-2000s, we all worked at Linden Lab, the creator of Second Life, one of the pioneering virtual worlds. While at Linden Lab, we effectively had remote teams. Our teams were in different locations, and so we had virtual meetings "in-world."[2] We set up offices around virtual campfires, inside castles or, for my office, a Bedouin tent at a desert oasis. During a meeting, we used chat and spatially accurate voice software – when someone on my virtual left spoke, the sound came through the left channel on my headphones. We conducted most of our work meetings that way, using virtual whiteboards and sharing slides within Second Life. We developed infrastructure to support these systems, so that we could coordinate our work across the company.

With that experience at Linden Lab at our disposal, Jen's travel schedule wasn't that disruptive or frightening for our new startup. Jen has a strong internal compass for integrity, so we knew she'd deliver on her commitments – and I'd better deliver on mine! We knew how to manage a virtual team already. So, we decided to start with an experiment – a Move to the Edge method – and learn how to conduct meetings via iteration until we had a successful "prototype." Our version emphasized weekly demos, aka "showing your work," that enabled fast feedback, increased alignment, and valued learning.

These concepts combine an experimental mindset (emphasis on learning) and growth mindset (emphasis on improving) and centers on a core of, "I don't know, and I'm curious to find out." As long as there is a clear assessment of risks and a mitigation strategy, it makes deciding to take a step against the grain much easier and much faster to course correct. Our criteria were simple – Jen would find apartments with high-speed internet, we'd iterate on our product, and we'd demo our work to each other weekly. If it didn't work, we'd know quickly and we'd figure out the right correction.

However, we knew we needed to focus on building systems that could sustain our company for the 18 months that Jen was abroad. Therefore, we built Declare It Center processes, starting with transparent work. The practice of transparency was primarily expressed in our use of communication and project tracking tools.[3] These tools help track progress of work, across any team, from the CEO to the newest employee. As a result, the tasks people are working on, the progress they are making, or their blocks to completing the task are visible artifacts of their work, without extra effort.

Combined with a daily standup meeting, teams keep aligned on tasks, highlight unexpected risks, and take direct immediate action when necessary. (A standup is a team meeting where each person describes what they were working on yesterday, what they are working on today, and any blockers to progress. Generally, these take no more than 10 minutes.)

While this method of working was very new to me personally, I adapted because of the ease it created in coordinating our work.

Creating ease is a core value of Declare It Center processes, and this helped us establish transparency as a core value at Truss. Starting from these practices, we continue to use Move to Edge methods to evolve our remote-first company, and we use Declare It Center infrastructure to share our processes with new employees and our clients.[4]

A decade later, we continue to make it work every day. By summer 2021, Truss is a fully distributed company with nearly 130 employees working in more than 30 states. Being distributed imposed unique challenges through every phase of growth, but we've iterated through many versions of software, infrastructure, communication platforms, video products, meeting protocols, and cultural norms to enable us to scale our company. What I couldn't anticipate is that what started as a method to solve the problem of our cofounder Jen traveling across Europe for 18 months would prove to be one of the best – and most prescient – business decisions we ever made.

We've used, discarded, or adapted a ton of Declare It Center processes over the last decade of being a remote-first company. This chapter highlights two of most important: retrospectives and Truss values. In Chapter 5, I include our updated Truss distributed playbook. That playbook contains detailed practices from how we conduct meetings to how we invest in employee effectiveness, so that you can benefit from some of our work as you consider remote, distributed, or hybrid work environments.

Retrospectives (Retros)

Retros are a practice we at Truss adapted from the UK Digital Service, for the purpose of dedicating time on a regular basis for teams to review their work. The meeting is structured so that problems are uncovered and discussed in a blameless fashion.

The power and distinction of this process versus other review processes is that well-run retros can cause a tidal shift in organizational culture away from "Whose fault is this?" to curiosity about "How did this happen?" Finally, great retros always generate specific, concrete action items, so that the investment in time is paid back with tangible activities that improve the team's performance.

Beyond the benefit of learning, the other benefit of retros is that it increases psychological safety.[5] Psychological safety is "a belief that one will not be punished or humiliated for speaking up with ideas, questions, concerns, or mistakes," according to Dr. Amy Edmonson, who coined the term. In her research, she finds this is a crucial component of high-functioning teams and companies. The Retro is an explicit practice of blameless learning and it is one of our most venerable Declare It Center practices at Truss. It allows us to systematize learning, scale with our growth, share the practice with our clients, and sustain the practice over almost 10 years. Let's go into some detail.

The best retros occur when the participants have a direct experience with the topic. For example, a product team would be best to review the impact of a new feature. However, it's often useful to have people from adjacent departments attend because the topic is likely to impact a wider array of people than only one group. For example, individuals from sales, business development, and client success could have valuable input in a product retro. Increasing the diversity of informed perspectives generally leads to higher-quality learning.

Choosing a cadence for retros is important, especially if you are trying to introduce this practice for the first time. When you're starting to introduce retrospectives into your organization, do them frequently: every two weeks until the retrospective starts to lack insightful, concrete conversation. Once people start to get comfortable with this format, increase the interval between retros to three weeks and see how that feels. Once everything is going smoothly, you'll end up with a retro every four to eight weeks, depending on how much is changing around your team.

Documentation is a key part of a successful retro, because it enables the team to track the action items that emerge, and it allows for other people outside the group to track progress and capture learnings that they can apply to their own team. This is a good example of the value of transparency.

Going back to the product feature example, other product teams can learn from the mistakes discussed in the retro too, especially if they are experiencing the same pattern of problems. It might lead to an insight that can improve the entire system.

Retros began as in-person experiences; however, we've adapted them as we've become a larger and remote-first company. At first, we held retros using a simple shared document, divided into the sections below, and participants copy-pasted their answers. Over a certain size, this became more cumbersome, so we've also experimented with a lot of different software tools. For us, Retrium works best, but there are other services that will work for your organization. Online services also enable attendees to submit their answers anonymously, which helps increase participation and candor.

If you have the opportunity for an in-person retro, use sticky notes, pens, and a whiteboard to create a rich, interactive experience.

Exercise: Hold a Retrospective

Since this is such an important Declare It Center process, I'm sharing our standard retrospective sequence as a practice exercise for you to conduct with your team. The entire exercise should take 90 minutes. This timeline includes an extra 10 minutes of slack so that you always end on time.

Before You Begin   Identify the facilitator and a note taker. The facilitator runs the meeting, makes sure it stays on track, and makes sure people are heard. The note taker makes sure possible ideas and actions are collected as the meeting progresses.

For remote meetings, the facilitator manages the order of speakers. At Truss, the facilitator uses what we call *the hand stack* in the Chat function. When attendees have a comment, they write "hand," "re" for a specific response, or "q" for clarifying questions. This enables the facilitator to manage the conversation flow, and the transparency of chat helps the group manage their own contributions. It is easy to see when one person is dominating the conversation!

For in-person meetings, only the note taker has a computer; the facilitator usually uses a smartphone timer for each section. Collect a bunch of markers and sticky notes and then book a room where your team will be undisturbed for 90 minutes.

Set the Scene (5 Minutes)   The facilitator should make sure everybody is in the room, settled, with screens and phones closed or laptops down. Remind everyone what's happened since the last retro and, if necessary, how the process works. If this is your first retro, this is a great time to walk through the entire process. It's okay if it takes more than five minutes; you won't have any actions to review in your first one.

Review Actions from Last Retro (5 Minutes)   Quickly go through actions from the last retro and confirm that they have been completed. If an action hasn't been completed, do not automatically carry it forward; it didn't get done for a reason. If it still matters, someone will almost certainly bring it up again.

Write Down the Good Stuff (10 Minutes)   Each person on the team should write down good things, with one item per Post-it, virtual or otherwise. Good things are: things that went particularly well, things that the team wants to continue doing, and things that the team wants to do more of. Aim to be concrete and specific whenever possible.

In a virtual setting, the facilitator can ask participants to write "done" in chat, or verbally check. Once folks are done writing their notes, the facilitator can reveal the answers in the retro software, ask folks to copy-paste into a shared document, or if in person, have attendees stick Post-its on a wall in the room. It's okay if folks finish early (although don't be too eager to cut a section short – you want people to have time to reflect).

Read Out Loud and Group Them (5 Minutes)   Read each entry / Post-it out loud, taking turns so that all members of the group are reading. This is important – at minimum, everyone wants to be heard and seen. Reading each entry / Post-it equalizes the contribution of all members of the group and minimizes the effect of the most senior or most voluble person in the room. Sharing the load of reading also recreates a sense of team. Reading the entry / Post-it out loud helps folks who learn better from listening than reading; it also allows people to clarify a thought if it was confusing.

The next step is to group entries or Post-its into whatever themes you find. It's common for a given team to have regular themes. As the group gets large – let's say over eight people – we've adopted a practice where one or two people take the lead on grouping. This gives other people a 3- to 5-minute break and allows for faster organization.

Vote on the Topics to Be Discussed (5 Minutes)   People get the same number of votes, usually three to seven, depending on the size of the group and the number of topics. These votes are represented in dot stickers, but we've used checkmarks, stars, and smiley faces. People can use all their votes on one theme or spread them around. In online settings, we do this anonymously, but it's not a requirement. Once complete, the themes with the most votes are discussed in order of the highest voted.

Discuss the Good (10 Minutes)   Have a group discussion about each theme. If your team is new, try going theme by theme and asking questions like:

- What should we keep doing?
- Why did these go well, and what can we learn?
- Are there actions that someone here can take?

Ideally, at the end of this time you've talked about a couple of the entries and have a few possible actions in your notes. You are not trying to talk about everything on the board at every retro, but you should be covering the most important elements in a theme.

At the end of the time, the notes, themes, votes, and actions should be captured and shared. For in-person retros, the note taker should take photos of the Post-its. These become valuable over time; being able to review retros for a team over a quarter can be a great way to see long-term trends or persistent items that never quite make it into the discussion.

Write Down the Bad Stuff (15 Minutes)   Yes, you spend more time on the bad than the good. This is because most of your improvements are going to come from discussing what didn't go well and how to fix them for the next time. It also keeps teams from being too focused on self-congratulations. Bad things are anything the team wants to stop happening or things that went poorly.

Once folks are done writing their Post-its, repeat the steps for Write Down the Good Stuff. It's okay if folks finish early, but be very cautious about cutting this section short. It can take a few minutes of people sitting and reflecting before something bad or challenging comes to mind.

Read the Sticky Notes Out Loud and Group Them (5 Minutes) Just like what you did in the good part. Your themes for the bad part don't have to be the same as the themes for the good part.

Discuss the Bad (15 Minutes) Have a group discussion about what's on the board. If your team is new, try going theme by theme and asking questions like:

- Can you elaborate on what didn't work well, from your perspective? (Note: It's important to recognize that what didn't work well for one person might be working great for another person. That distinction can contain an enormous amount of value, especially in identifying blind spots in the organization.)
- Can we work out why these went badly?
- Can we work out what we need to do to improve matters or prevent specific things from happening?
- Are there actions that someone here could take?

It can be uncomfortable to discuss the bad stuff. The facilitator should be aware of the mood of the room and encourage candor without blame. Radical candor is the method and psychological safety is the foundation; a high-functioning team can tell each other when they've failed without things getting ugly. It can take a while to get there; don't worry if your first retro only has complaints about uncontroversial items.

At the end of the time, the notes, themes, votes, and actions should be captured and shared. For in-person retros, the note taker should take photos of the Post-its.

Discuss and Assign Potential Actions (10 Minutes) The note taker should go through each possible action that was collected in the retro. For each action, the team should make sure everyone understands it, decide if they want to do it, and, if so, assign someone present to complete it, ideally by the next retrospective.

It's not unreasonable to have 5–10 actions from this meeting, ranging in severity from "Please ask Facilities to raise the temperature in here because we're freezing" to "Work with the Security team to make sure our deployment process doesn't expose unprotected secrets on our laptops." Track those actions the same way you'd track project work.

Afterward The facilitator and note taker should put the notes, photos, and action items in a well-known place where the team can retrieve them later. People outside the team can also track what was discussed, learned, and acted upon.

Evolving Retros

We used to have all-company retros when we were less than 30 people, about company-wide issues. Most Trussels had enough context for each other's work to make retros a useful exercise for everyone. Retros could be for specific events, like a quarterly meeting, or a policy like salary transparency. However, when we went through a growth spurt in 2018–2020, retros were not as effective. Fewer people had context about a specific event, we were moving toward more specialists, and there is simply less air time when there are 60 people instead of 20. We realized retros are most effective when the team who was actively involved in the topic is centered, has enough time to explore topics in depth, and is capable of committing to the action steps that emerge. We've paused the all-company retro, and we're still debating how to achieve the same kind of high-value, low-effort, blameless learning for company-wide issues.

That said, we continue to have smaller team, project, or event retros, both within Truss and with our clients. At its best, introducing retros to our clients increases trust between teams, and it often accelerates better outcomes because it creates a venue for improvement that didn't previously exist at the client. It is an impactful Declare It Center process, whether your company is remote or not. Systematizing psychological safety, scaling trust, and sustaining an ethos of constant improvement is an incredible foundation for building a company capable of responding to uncertain and complex situations.

Premortems

"Put yourself nine months in the future. The project we're about to start is an absolute failure. Looking back, what went wrong?"

That's the core prompt for a premortem, which happens after a project or leadership team has specified goals, metrics, resources, and a roadmap, but before the project begins. This technique was developed by Gary Klein in 2007 to reduce the frequency of project failure. Earlier research indicated that this type of technique increases the ability to correctly identify reasons for future outcomes by 30 percent.[6] Applying that finding, the premortem asks project team members to imagine project failures in a way that enables mitigating actions to take place in advance. For Truss, it's remarkable how many times teams uncover a missing step, communication, or resource that wasn't considered before.

There are many different ways to prompt the question, but we tend to keep it simple. Ask the question and give everyone 7–10 minutes to write their answers. Then each person reads their answers to the group while the facilitator records the notes. The team either votes a priority list or, more frequently, engages in a discussion about how to mitigate the imagined points of failure. Action steps are assigned, and that's it.

What I love about premortems is that they can be perversely fun. Encouraging people to imagine worst-case scenarios without blame often creates moments of laughter ("This will fail because Everett's calendar is blocked for three weeks – again"), and the freedom to indulge in real and fantastical scenarios. Along with the serious assessment of consequential risk, premortems are essentially a creative exercise, and they usually leave the team with higher energy and confidence. Premortems can be used during a Move to the Edge phase, but because they are a core part of our infrastructure at this point, I put it in the Declare It Center section of the framework.

Truss Values

Values are an important part of building a sustainable culture. As you might expect, we think of this as an opportunity to make it part of our Declare It Center infrastructure. Specifically, the act of writing values down, making them explicit, and sharing with the company is *cultural* infrastructure. Our story is an interesting example of how Declare It Center methods can enable evolution and improvements to culture by anyone in the organization.

My cofounders and I decided to write our values down early in our company history. Each of us had experiences of being part of distinct, strong, organizational cultures. We all came from Linden Lab, which conceived of the Tao of Linden, a set of values that provided useful guidance for all the Lindens, as employees were called. I had been part of strong work cultures at Ninth House Network, Self-Help, Bain & Company, while my most successful soccer teams had strong values that we worked to uphold.

However, we were explicit about two things that were different:

1. We wanted to write them down. Explicit values are an explicit marker about what is important, and if done well, can evolve as the company grows.

2. We wanted them to be verbs instead of nouns, concepts, or ideas. "Improve by marginal gains" is much more grounded than "high performance." If we were successful, our values would repel the wrong people as much as attract the right people, which is the outcome that is best for everyone.

Finally, they were written such that a new person coming to Truss, or a Trussel who encounters a new situation, can use the values to guide their thinking and their actions. We got them done over six weeks, meeting each Wednesday for three hours after work with a writing facilitator, until we hammered out six core values, with three supporting principles underneath (see Figure 3.1).

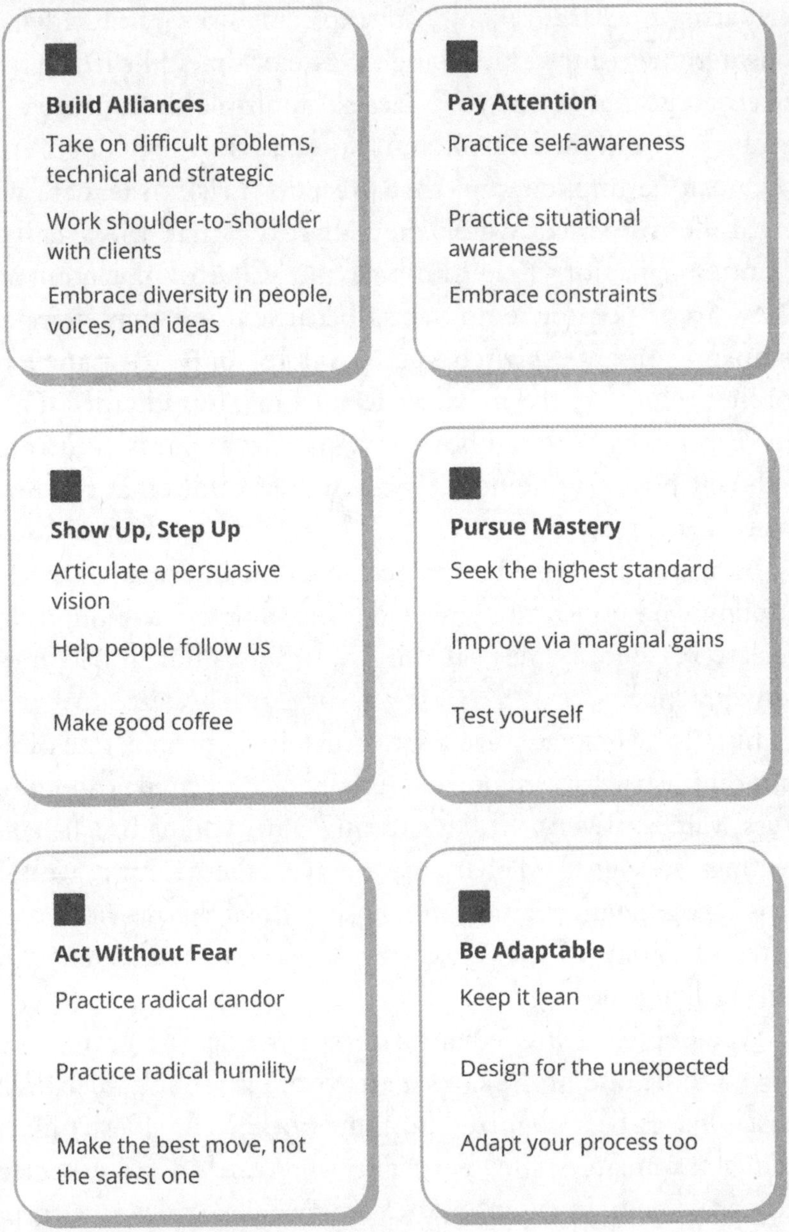

Build Alliances

Take on difficult problems, technical and strategic

Work shoulder-to-shoulder with clients

Embrace diversity in people, voices, and ideas

Pay Attention

Practice self-awareness

Practice situational awareness

Embrace constraints

Show Up, Step Up

Articulate a persuasive vision

Help people follow us

Make good coffee

Pursue Mastery

Seek the highest standard

Improve via marginal gains

Test yourself

Act Without Fear

Practice radical candor

Practice radical humility

Make the best move, not the safest one

Be Adaptable

Keep it lean

Design for the unexpected

Adapt your process too

FIGURE 3.1 The Truss values

Back in 2012, many startup investors and advisors considered writing values to be a waste of time. I heard, "Grow fast, then go figure out your values," multiple times. However, if values are not made explicit, it doesn't mean they don't exist. They can be implicit, and that presents a risk to leaders who might be surprised when they discover that their culture tolerates behaviors that diminish the value of the company. They are risky for employees because they may join the company for an expected set of values, only to realize the implicit values are the most powerful and contradictory. There is a reason why "the old boys club" is a vivid phrase – it refers to the unspoken, ephemeral, yet powerful values that can make or break a career.

An action that enables a repeatable outcome, enables people to follow, and transforms a new idea into a practice – sounds like Declare It Center! The real story, however, is how it becomes a living practice.

In 2015, when we were approximately 15 people, one of our senior infrastructure engineers, Jeremy, shared an idea about our Truss values. Every Friday, during our company all-hands meeting, he suggested that at the end of the meeting, we take turns recognizing one person whose actions the previous week represented one of the Truss values. Values shout-outs?! This was a brilliant idea!

We adopted it immediately, and in the last six years, it has evolved to be one of the favorite parts of everyone's week. Who doesn't like to be recognized for their work? Who doesn't like to make a teammate smile, especially when they don't expect it? Wins all around. In addition, it's a practice that scales as we grow, is easy to follow, and serves to reinforce cultural values with very little individual effort. It's a perfect example of Declare It Center infrastructure.

Case Study: How We Made Salaries Transparent (Declare It Center)

Declare It Center processes help organizations systematize, scale, share, and sustain their solutions to complex problems. In this section, I briefly share the processes we used to turn our Move to the Edge – salary transparency – into a system. You might note that some of the practices seem "ordinary," and you would be correct. That's the point – turning something innovative into something ordinary is the effect of good Declare It Center design.

Center Question	Declare It Center Practice
How do we attract and train?	Decisions records, recruiting playbook
How do we measure and be accountable?	Recruiting, hiring, retention data
How do we maintain trust?	Policy, launch system design
How do we stay current on compensation?	Compensation committee
What are the unknown unknowns?	Retrospectives

Many of the specific practices above are also detailed in Chapter 6. The additional step we made is to put the infrastructure for measurement into the hands of the team that is accountable for delivering results – the hiring and recruiting team – while building systems to make sure the results are transparent to the organization so that we keep ourselves accountable. Similarly, we created a compensation committee, comprised of people from different parts of the organization. Serving terms of six months, their job is to make sure that compensation is equitable. As always, we embed periodic retrospectives to make sure we identify new issues and provide an avenue for new improvements.

As of summer 2021, we are 125 people, and we've scaled this system to accommodate that growth. Our hypotheses have been validated by experience and by outside research. For instance, gender pay gap shrinks when companies are required to disclose them.[7] We've added a variety of different processes, as well as realized the benefits – unexpected benefits – for things like hiring and recruiting, which were much smoother and much more efficient.

There are new challenges that we are currently iterating on, specifically about expanding our rubrics to incorporate more levels, especially with leadership. "This is something that we actually started running into as we scaled the organization. When we first created the rubric, we were only about 20 people. So the distinctions between levels were clearer because we were a smaller organization, and there were only a few people that were very senior. It didn't require much detailed breakdown or nuanced breakdown," says my cofounder Jen, who architected the rollout. "As we've scaled to 120 people, we have a larger leadership team, which means we need more clarity around levels *within* leadership." In expanding our leadership rubrics, we've followed many of the same Declare It Center steps like retros to seek and act on issues to improve our Salary Transparency system.

When I opened the Salary Transparency case study with a (fake) business card with salary listed on it, would you have predicted that instead of creating controversy, a transparent salary process would lead to someone potentially advocating on your behalf to get paid more? We didn't either, but because we built good Declare It Center processes, we've been able to sustain this innovation in order to achieve the outcomes we wanted: a solution to the complex problem of salary disparities along gender and race.

Case Study: Healthcare.gov

In October 2013, I was cleaning the dinner table of stray cheese tortellini that had missed the mouth of my seven-year-old daughter when I heard my cell phone ring. It was 7 p.m. on a

Sunday. I don't expect calls then, but I was curious enough to check my screen.

It said, "Mark Ferlatte," and I felt my breath stop.

Mark is one of my cofounders of Truss. If you are a founder, leader, or executive, you know that when you get a call from your colleague on a Sunday evening, it's not going to be good news. I answered my phone, dreading the ruin of my nice fall weekend.

"Hey, what's up?"

"Welllll . . . I have some news," said Mark, in a tone offering to soften the blow yet succeeding to ratchet up the tension. "I just got invited to join the team fixing Healthcare.gov. My contact told me, 'I could get the CTO of the United States to call you, but seriously, just show up.'"

I paused for three beats, long enough for an expletive to be voiced in my head.

I said, "You gotta go."

"Yeah, I'm gonna go."

"When are you going to leave?"

"On Tuesday," he replied.

"Okay. Jen and I will figure it out."

The entire conversation with Mark lasted about 90 seconds. More importantly, we made a decision, with little information, significant risk, and major consequence, in 90 seconds.

Let me back up for a second to give some context. In 2010, 14 months into his first term in office, US President Barack Obama signed the Patient Protection and Affordable Care Act (ACA).[8] Healthcare reform was going to be the signature legacy of Obama's domestic policy agenda, and in signing the bill, he put into motion a series of political, legal, and administrative shifts that continue to reverberate over a decade later.

The bill also mandated a sweeping change in the delivery of healthcare insurance. For the first time, the federal government would create a healthcare exchange website, called Healthcare .gov, that would facilitate the sale of private health insurance for residents of the United States. Individuals could search, register, choose, and confirm healthcare coverage for themselves and their families. CGI Federal, a federal IT contractor, was given the contract to build the site, and subsequently farmed out the task to 55 subcontractors to complete the work.[9]

The site launched on October 1, 2013, and promptly crashed. Instead of the 50,000 expected visitors, the site received 250,000 visitors on the first day.[10] The system was not designed to respond to the increased capacity. In fact, when the team analyzed the site capacity later, they estimated that the system could have only handled 50 simultaneous users.[11] The crash highlighted other problems with the system, which made fixing the basic functions of the site extremely difficult. Over the next few weeks, the Obama Administration scrambled to figure out what happened while trying to stave off the frenzy of political opposition that threatened the entirety of his legislation. The president convened a new executive task force with authority to bring in the outside technology experts in order to save the site – which I learned on that Sunday phone call.

Those seconds fundamentally changed the trajectory of our company, but we didn't know that at the time. In fact, none of us knew exactly what "fixing Healthcare.gov" even meant. There was no contract, no timeline, no negotiations, no roadmap. The only thing that was certain was that if Healthcare.gov could not sign up 1 million people, via the website or the call center, by December 24, 2013, Congress was authorized to revoke it.

How could we say yes to such an important, potentially disastrous decision? We didn't know it yet, but we were already starting to practice the principles that became Move to the Edge, Declare It Center.

"Here's an address of a hotel, near Baltimore. Fly there, find the conference room, and they'll tell you what to do." That sounds more like the start of *Ocean's 11* than an invitation to join one the most pivotal public software projects of the early twenty-first century. No contract, no scope of work, no salary, no office, no team roster, no title and no role – how does that rank on the scale of uncertainty?

That's how our involvement in Healthcare.gov started – on the Edge. Mark joined the new 30-person ad hoc team while Jen Leech and I managed our fledgling startup. Mark and the team had one clear certainty – the Healthcare.gov website had to register 1 million people in 60 days, or Congress had the mandate to rescind the Affordable Care Act (ACA). Given a Republican-led Congress opposed to President Barack Obama's landmark legislation, the ACA would be killed unless the ad hoc team hit that goal.

There are many reasons why $200 million was spent on a piece of software that registered a grand total of six people before crashing on day one. I'm going to focus on one reason in particular – the mismatch of a complicated approach to a complex problem. The procurement office and the contractor approached developing Healthcare.gov software – for registering millions of new people – as a *complicated* problem. That is, linear, well-understood, predictable interactions that could be managed from a centralized, command-and-control operational model. The 55 contractors were each given their parts to execute, with the assumption that all the parts would fit together as long as they followed the contract.

Except this was a *complex* problem. The previous vendor teams followed their contracts, but when the site launched, it crashed almost immediately. The software was designed to accommodate an average number of registrations per minute, but hundreds of thousands of people logged into the site, and it crashed under the load. No one accounted for the complex problem of human curiosity. In fact, no one interviewed potential customers to understand their needs and behaviors to factor that into the design of the site. The increased load amplified negative effects on the entire system – a classic feature of complex problems that we nicknamed *the fractal* – an endless cascade of brokenness that seemed to multiply in unpredictable ways.

The fractal wasn't confined to how the software behaved. The approach to managing the project followed the complicated playbook. Command central dictated how the software was to be developed, far away from the front-line developers of that software. If the developers wanted to get information, they had to drive a few hours from the main software development offices to the operations center.[12] As a result, as developers encountered unknowns, they had to go through multiple levels of approval to investigate or make changes. When teams are governed by a complicated problem-solving mindset, discovery is treated as deviance. In this case, deviance required contract modifications and several layers of approval. You can imagine that the discovery of unknowns – a necessary practice for reducing risk while solving complex problems – was unwelcome and thus undocumented. Multiply that by 55 separate contractors, and you have the setting for a massive and embarrassing failure.

The ad hoc team brought in a new set of some of the top engineers in the country, with diverse perspectives and skills. Diversity is a key practice for dealing with complex problems because it increases the probability of discovering unknowns. This diverse team had a common set of practices, starting with a simple question: "What problem do we have?" Rather than assuming they understood the problem, they had the curiosity and humility to acknowledge that they didn't. "I don't know" is a critical step in complex problem solving, because it launches the practice of discovery in order to move forward. As a result, they didn't start at the center with the executives and policymakers. They Moved to the Edge – to the engineers on the front lines, who had the daily experience of outages, bugs, new and legacy systems that prevented the site from functioning.

They looked into the monitoring system to learn about basic questions, but unfortunately, the system wasn't able to answer basic questions like, "What is the latency of the site?" "What is the percentage of errors?" or even fundamental questions like, "How many people are able to progress from starting the application through to completing the application?"

When they dug deeper, they couldn't figure out whether the steps they were taking were actually helping. This is another critical step for addressing a complex problem. If you misunderstand the complexity of a system, then you risk optimizing for the wrong thing and causing greater harm in another part of a system. Make several of these decisions, and you are condemned to an endless game of whack-a-mole. By pausing to ask this question, it opened up a different practice that became crucial for making progress.

This new team took their inspiration from Maslow's Hierarchy of Needs. Mikey Dickerson, one of the ad hoc team leaders, said, "If we're working on a higher quality of problem this week than we were last week, then we're making progress." The model doesn't presume that the team knows the answer, but they can document if they're working on higher-level problems (Figure 3.2).

For example, they added a functional monitoring system – and in the first days, it told them horrible things about the performance of the site. But this bad news didn't make the team freeze or flee. Instead, they adapted their plan and set a baseline for the bottom rung of the problem hierarchy. This updated hierarchy created focus and a common language. In doing so, it enabled Dickerson to realize that the initial efforts to fix the

Maslow's Hierarchy

Dickerson's Hierarchy of Reliability

FIGURE 3.2   Dickerson's Hierarchy of Reliability, based on Maslow's Hierarchy of Needs

problem were at the wrong end of the hierarchy. The problem hierarchy is an example of building infrastructure, a practice that is key to the Declare It Center process. This hierarchy was scalable, sharable, and sustainable, enabling even new members of the team to learn and take action within hours of arriving.

A problem hierarchy is a clever practice that enables people to focus their efforts, make progress, enhance transparency, and incorporate new perspectives toward solving a complex problem. How do you determine what is a higher-level problem? Mark says, "What problem do I wish I was working on, instead of being stuck by this crappy problem I have now?" The practice of asking questions like this is part of a Declare It Center infrastructure that organizations can apply in a variety of contexts. The problem hierarchy for your day, your team, and your company will vary – but the question will reveal the priority of unknowns and actions relevant to your complex problem. Reliability is the desired and achievable result.

Problem hierarchy established, transparency elevated, monitors installed. Now for the next issue: Many of the engineers already had ideas to solve problems plaguing the site, but they couldn't take action. Contract language and management practice was rooted in the complicated problem-solving framework of command-and-control. The assumption is that the commander (an executive four to five levels removed from the action) understands the problem and the ground troops' (aka the front-line engineers') job is simply to carry out orders. Unfortunately, this was a misapplication of a complicated mindset to a complex problem.

The leaders of the ad hoc team went to the executives with a clear proposal: Enable the problem-solvers to take action without needing commander approval. The ad hoc leaders would ensure that executives would get transparent reporting on progress and outcomes, enabling the ad hoc team to solve problems without interference while focusing on the core outcome. Their proposal was approved and, combined with the transparent monitoring system, they created the War Room.

The War Room was another core piece of Declare It Center infrastructure. It was the center of where all the action was happening, run by a "pit boss." The pit boss had the authority to spin up or shut down the website – at any time, for any reason – to ensure that the ultimate goal was met.

Their practices were put to the test when the team was putting the site through a full four-hour restart. At 9:30 a.m., Mark got a call from the White House. "President Obama is appearing on CNN at 2:00 p.m. Will the website be working?" If that call had come two weeks earlier, a positive answer would have been in doubt. However, Mark and the team had made website restarts a regular, transparent, operational practice, iterating through their problem hierarchy until they started to get reliable results. Despite the unexpected, high-pressure call and the low margin of error, the answer was "Yes."

Using these practices, the team surpassed the milestone of 1 million people registered by December 24, 2013. By the close of enrollment, 7 million American citizens had healthcare through Healthcare.gov. The team remained working on the site from October through March 2014 and then a new group of companies, including our company, Truss, began working the 2.0 version. As of April 2020, 11.4 million people were enrolled through Healthcare.gov and state-based exchanges, and cumulatively 27 million people have enrolled since the inception of the program.

What Did We Learn? Changing Mindsets Requires Changing Systems

Solving the complex problem of the Healthcare.gov website was a major achievement. However, the more lasting impact was revealing fundamental problems in the procurement of software by government agencies.

According to The Standish Report, 87 percent of government IT contracts over $6M fail.[13] There are myriad causes, but one of them is rooted in the framing of problems and solutions as *complicated*. This framing is, essentially, "We understand the problem; your job is to execute the plan." The framing is enshrined into requirements, statements of work, and other government contract language. The traditional contracting officer, procurement officer, and software vendors would make agreements to develop the software. But many of these agreements assume that the problem is well understood and they can apply "tried-and-true" methods. Unfortunately, the legacy of the old saying, "Nobody ever got fired for buying IBM," can still hold sway over some IT decision-makers.[14]

However, like General Stanley McCrystal detailed in his book *Team of Teams*, when the problems in Iraq changed from complicated to complex, even the most powerful, well-trained force could be made vulnerable, brittle, and ineffectual. Acknowledgment of unknowns is a fundamental requirement for dealing with complexity, but is anathema to the command-control complicated model developed in factories in the nineteenth and twentieth centuries. The reality of modern software is that the promise of speed, convenience, accessibility, and scale comes with the risk of new interaction patterns that have unforeseen consequences. When the management of modern software remains stuck in a complicated framework, we have the setting for the classic mismatch that begat a website that broke within hours of launch.

Contrast this with the Move to the Edge, Declare It Center practices used to fix Healthcare.gov. The Move to the Edge practice of diversity was represented in the multitude of skills on the teams, from security, to application engineering, infrastructure, operations, design, and delivery. This diversity facilitates better problem-solving, innovation, and reduces blind spots. Using the Move to the Edge practice of iterative, "sprint" development instead of "waterfall" development, the team surfaced unknowns, new data, or unexpected issues. Engaging customers – from collecting needs, testing responses to gathering feedback – is a fundamental practice of centering the human experience as valuable and desirable. The visibility of these practices, and the success of the results for Healthcare.gov, kickstarted the movement to reform and rebuild procurement infrastructure for federal and state governments.

Declare It Center in Modern Government

Despite the transformations that resulted from a Move to the Edge, Declare It Center approach to modern software development, there's a long way to go – because the issue is complex. There are other examples of systemic failure: (1) the botched $617 million United Health Infrastructure Program in the State of Rhode Island;[15] (2) the failure of the state of Texas's rigid energy infrastructure to respond to a winter storm in February 2021 that caused at least 58 deaths, $18 billion in damages, and an overcharge of $16 billion in utility bills;[16] and (3) the failed rollout of the COVID vaccine distribution network by the CDC.[17]

This latest software failure is worth examining using a Move to the Edge, Declare It Center framework. On the software development side, Deloitte repurposed proprietary software – a classic complicated practice – to solve a complex delivery problem. On the procurement side, according to the *New York Times*, the CDC awarded the contract to Deloitte using a no-bid process (a noncompetitive bid) while rejecting a solution that had been purpose-built by a Black woman who is an expert in vaccine distribution.[18]

Did CDC react to uncertainty by falling back on the familiar, even as states warned them about the inadequacy of Deloitte's solution? Why was a no-bid process used to award proprietary software, when transparency and open information flow are a critical practice for responding to a complex crisis that has cost millions of lives?

Instead, imagine using a Move to the Edge, Declare It Center practice of small experiments such as live competitive demos, and insisting on customer interviews to ensure that the project addresses their needs. Imagine removing statutes that require "onsite" development in favor of diversifying vendors and taking advantage of the move toward distributed and remote work.

This vision is not fanciful. Starting with the Government Digital Services in the UK (Uk.gov) in 2012, teams have been moving to the edge, experimenting and iterating on practices, and declaring it center with artifacts documenting their methods. This inspired the creation of United States Digital Service (USDS) in 2014, the first public agency in the US dedicated to these new practices. This model spread to state and local governments in the United States, like the New Jersey Office of Innovation. Internationally, Estonia committed to a digital service as a fundamental part of governance, prompting innovations like E-Residency and E-Identity in 2015.

Playbooks and guidebooks documented how leaders could use Move to the Edge practices to adapt to complexity by creating useful, impactful services for citizens through public agencies. One of those that influenced me personally was the Digital Services Playbook, endorsed by the Federal CIO.[19] Early on, it was a big struggle to document these novel approaches without the overwhelming abstract policy language typical of most public documents. Jennifer Pahlka, founder of Code for America, and one of the originating authors of the *Digital Services Playbook*, told me, "Ryan Panchadsaram deserves an enormous amount of credit. He drove the commitment to write in simple, direct actionable language." Despite that, "I left feeling like a complete failure on that front, and it wasn't until probably about a year later that I realized that people were actually using it. Now I feel incredibly proud of it."

Even more influential were the changes to the procurement rules that guide how public agencies can buy software or contract with companies to build custom software for specific targeted use. The rescue of Healthcare.gov demonstrated that smaller teams, using modern software practices, operating in remote locations, can deliver results. Before then, requirements to be "on location" effectively blocked newer, smaller companies from competing for work. On-location requirements favor large companies who can afford to split their teams, whether or not they are the best choice for delivering the work. The successful practice of iteration was manifested in the decreased length of contracts. Before, it was assumed that an initiative that might last seven years required a seven-year contract worth hundreds of millions or billions of dollars. Despite the rapid pace of technology, government contracting officers (COs) felt bound to commit to one company and their subcontractors for the entire seven years. Instead, the new mindset of agile software enabled COs to split the work into reasonable time frames, which enabled greater competition, lower risks, and the ability to adopt new software technologies.

Now, organizations such as 18F, the Digital Service Coalition, Code for America, and others partner with contracting officers and policymakers. They illustrate how to create the environment where the right problems can be identified, and the right experiments can be tested. There is emerging research and practice changing how we measure progress from "How many widgets per hour are you producing?" to "What kind of outcomes are you delivering, for whom, and at what level of quality?" As a result, there are more leaders and decision makers who recognize that we are in an era of complex systems, and our approaches need to shift. "I had no strategy for it, but I knew I was part of a larger transformation, not just a *Digital Services Playbook*," Jennifer continued, reflecting on her role.

Finally, we are seeing the emergence of companies designed for complexity from the start. Veterans of the Healthcare.gov project started companies like Truss, Ad Hoc, and Fearless, among others. Unencumbered by the legacies rooted in command-control mindsets, these companies can deliver software systems with positive, measurable outcomes – often at a fraction of the cost. These companies and their counterparts within federal, state, and local governments are declaring that citizens – especially during a pandemic – deserve human-centered, accessible, adaptable software that delivers on the promised outcomes.

Case Study: Beyond the Scope: Responding to the California Wildfires

As the winds weaken aloft, gravity will take over as the primary vertical transport of the smoke. Suspended smoke will descend closer to the surface and could lead to darker skies and worsening air quality today. This is beyond the scope of our models so we rely on your reports!

- National Weather Service, San Francisco Bay Area, Twitter post, Sept. 9, 2020

"I began working in emergency response back in 2017 with the Tubbs Fire and then the Camp Fire. Since then, I've deployed on average four times per year," said my friend Jana. I've known Jana[20] for almost 10 years, but this was the first time I realized the level of her commitment as a native Californian, volunteering to support some of the biggest disasters in California history. "My primary role is to set up and manage large-scale emergency shelters for people who are displaced during large-scale wildfires."

The Tubbs Fire of 2017 and the Camp Fire of 2018 happen to be the two most destructive fires in California history, in terms of structures destroyed and fatalities.[21] At the time, 2017 and 2018 fires destroyed 1.5 million and 1.97 million acres, respectively, the largest in California history – until 2020, which destroyed 1.67 million acres by August. "When I got there, it was a Level Seven emergency.[22] I was in the Greater Chico Area, working the night shift. Because the scale had increased so much, there were only three of us to manage a shelter of 300 people. It was very clear this was way beyond the scale that people had planned for."

I'm from regions in the East Coast where we live through destructive snowstorms and hurricanes. What became apparent is that from a disaster-response perspective, we can prepare in advance for some of those events. There are predictive weather patterns and sophisticated models to help responders coordinate resources, plan strategies, and attempt to predict the path of landfall. Wildfires, on the other hand, don't have warning times. Response teams were trained to respond immediately, and their systems were optimized for random, sudden fire events.

According to Jana, what dawned on them after the 2018 Camp Fire is that the model had to be changed. California now had a *fire season*. "We have to figure out what works for us this time because this is going come up for us again," recalled Jana in her conversations with fire and shelter leaders. Just like Daniella in the early days of COVID, even with well-practiced systems, complexity can scale beyond expectations. Sometimes you can Move to the Edge, and sometimes you get Moved to the Edge.

I asked her to describe the first nights up at the Tubbs Fire. "My team arrived up there – there's just the three of us – and we all deployed there at one shelter for the entire two weeks working night shift. Three or four days after the start of the fire, we started noticing signs of Norovirus – basically the stomach flu – resulting in vomiting and diarrhea for a few days. The big problem is that it's highly contagious. Most of the shelters had evacuees that were symptomatic." On top of the displacement and tragedy of losing homes, families started having this outbreak, adding another level of discomfort and stress to an already very-stressed-out population. Her response team wasn't fully prepped with knowledge about a Norovirus, either, and as a result, she said, "All the staff shelters where we were staying at had it."

Jana continued, "Luckily, before we had left, I talked to a nurse, and she was actually talking to me about Norovirus in passing. I had a couple of printouts of procedures she used. But then she brought out a box of rubber gloves and asked me, 'Do you know what this is? No? Well, starting today you're going to carry these masks around. They're called PPE.' After showing me how Norovirus is transmitted and how to protect myself, she closed with, 'As soon as you get back to staff quarters, no matter how tired you are, you shower, wipe everything down, and wash your hands every single time.' When I started seeing symptoms, I thought, this kinda sounds a lot like what that nurse was talking about."

She and one of her co-leaders were the only ones who didn't get sick. A lucky break, an experiment, and a clear result. What's the Declare It Center process? The organization does blameless postmortems. They evaluate and share experiences after every deployment. Since it's over 90 percent volunteers, they have to create the psychological safety to enable those volunteers to offer their experience of what worked and what didn't. It's clear that everyone is deeply committed to getting better so they can serve their communities in crisis.

"Two years later, I was one of the people who was asked to talk about how we should respond during COVID." She shared her experience of learning during those unprecedented fires. "Personally, I've been on the Norovirus crusade since 2018. I advise my teams to bring their own supply of gloves and PPE, and I personally don't deploy without a gallon of bleach in the car." She's training herself and her team for the unknown.

Declare It Center to Sustain Your Work

Thus far, the case studies have illustrated different aspects of Declare It Center. Salary transparency was an example of systematizing the original innovation into normal operations. Healthcare.gov was an example of sharing a methodology – agile development – to not only solve an immediate problem but also influence the system of buying software at government agencies. Beyond the Scope was an illustration of using blameless postmortems to share an innovation to prevent forest fire evacuees from getting COVID.

The next case study is an example of using Declare It Center processes to scale an approach to complex problems with an unexpected but lasting result.

Case Study: World Central Kitchen

One of the critical aspects of Declare It Center is taking insights, innovations, and learnings from Move to the Edge and enabling them to become part of "normal" operations. It requires being intentional about building processes that enable others to follow. In the first case study of World Central Kitchen, Nate Mook detailed how they engage with people directly to develop hypotheses about the critical needs for nourishment, and the resources available to address them. But I was curious about how they are able to repeat that in different crises, countries, and scale it around the globe.

First, they train their staff and teams on the big picture – WCK has built a unique network in the restaurant and chef community around the globe, which connects them to capacity, production, facilities, suppliers, farmers, and other producers of food. "Jose Andres, our founder, jokes that we have kitchens everywhere in the world," says Nate, adding that they own none of them. When they first arrive at a crisis location, they simultaneously arrange support architecture and fundamental resources – kitchens, food suppliers, equipment, and transportation – so they are ready to deploy once they understand the critical needs on the ground. In addition, other services like data access, mapping, and finance are engaged, making sure the pathways to deliver information, location-based services, and money are cleared. Helping staff learn how to engage this network creates shared understanding that can be replicated, no matter the location.

Second, they show staff how to engage local leadership. They identify government and elected officials, NGOs (nongovern-mental organizations), and community leaders, each of whom has distinct and diverse knowledge that is crucial to identifying local needs. Not only does that diversify the sources of knowledge about preexisting resources, but it connects WCK to diverse sets of infrastructure that will be crucial for organizing the best response.

Third, they build an entire curriculum, including checklists and streams of work, to train people about what to do – and especially what questions to ask when they hit the ground. These three components enable WCK staff to implement their unique model, under high stress and uncertainty, *without knowing the answer.* "This gives us the ability to move quickly, anywhere in the world, even when we don't have a preexisting relationship." It's a brilliant example of building Declare It Center processes to support Move to the Edge methods.

Earlier, I explored how World Central Kitchen uses methods of Move to the Edge to navigate complex crisis response situations, and processes of Declare It Center to build tools and infrastructure to enable the organization to respond quickly in different parts of the world. But as we continued to talk, he described an unexpected use of the framework, which had profound implications for WCK's future.

"At the beginning of the pandemic, Jose and I were aghast at the global scale of it," began Nate, reflecting what a lot of us felt in that period between February and May 2020. They could see it was going to be massive, and with vaccines still months away, they were uncertain about how to respond to all the calls for assistance from around the world.

"It was a moment where we had to make a decision," he recalled. Historically, they would go to the location, assess the situation, set up kitchens, and start cooking. All the labor was handled by paid WCK staff, plus local chefs and restaurant workers, rather than volunteers. This was the core of a very successful model for disaster relief. However, the problem was that the scale of the pandemic was going to simultaneously affect multiple locations, and WCK didn't have enough staff to respond. So they questioned their own assumptions and developed a new hypothesis.

"What if we weren't doing all the cooking?"

Nate and Jose realized that they built a worldwide network of kitchens, chefs, suppliers, and servers already, but they had always insisted on doing the cooking themselves. Instead, what if they used local kitchens, chefs, and servers as the primary delivery of nourishment in communities after a disaster? This became their new hypothesis for meeting the unknown scale of the pandemic. They began to test it immediately.

They asked their network of chefs and kitchens if they had the capacity and the willingness to partner with them. The chefs were up for it, but the next challenge became coordination. They realized they needed to create a more distributed model and identify a local lead to coordinate the activity. "We decided to only focus on local kitchens and restaurants, not the national chains" as part of the network. They were exploring the Edge of their business model, yet they continued to be anchored on core principles: nourishment, local leadership, sustainable livelihoods, adaptability, and fast response.

Finally, they had to determine if the finances would work. This was a bold move on their part. Most disaster response rests on the assumption of providing the most relief – food, shelter, water, and medicine, among others – at the lowest possible cost. This echoes the complicated approach to problem solving that we explored in the Introduction. First, assume that people, food, transport, and delivery interact in a well-understood, linear way. Second, calculate and optimize the ratio of needs, costs, and time, then put the plan into action. This can be done from a command-center or headquarters far away, and put into operation anywhere, anytime.

But disasters are inherently complex! Damage from hurricanes varies from block to block, trailer park to gated neighborhood. People aren't stationary objects. They flee to other cities, gather at high grounds that only the locals know, and communicate through both official and unofficial channels. Food supplies might be destroyed, inaccessible, or untouched. Thus, we have a classic example of a decision-making based on complicated models being mismatched to the complex problem of disaster response. What's the result? With Hurricane Katrina, the result was thousands of empty FEMA trailers shipped to inaccessible locations while unhoused residents suffered in horrible conditions. In Puerto Rico, the result was millions of barely edible MREs delivered to locations that didn't need them.

WCK decided to raise money from donors with a different approach to a complex problem – how to provide nourishing meals to people suffering from the pandemic while providing ongoing livelihoods to kitchens and restaurateurs suffering from the lack of customers. Their ask: Instead of spending $2 or $3 per meal, they would spend $10, with the $7 difference going to local chefs, kitchens, and food suppliers to cook, serve, and rebuild.

"I didn't know if it would work, to be honest," said Nate, pausing as he retraced those uncertain days in the spring of 2020, "yet there I was, talking to the *Washington Post* about how we would make it work." It was a bold vision – $10 million at $10 per meal. They kept raising money for the vision, and by the end of 2020, they had raised $150 million using the new model, recycled through communities hit by the pandemic.

This is going to be the WCK model for the future – both for the pandemic and for disaster relief from hurricanes in Louisiana and wildfires in Greece. By following their model of asking great questions of local people, forming hypotheses that adapt to the situation at hand, and amassing flexible resources from a global network, WCK has made a significant impact on disaster-struck regions. These are all methods embodied in Move to the Edge. By building systems to train staff and local leaders, creating networks of kitchens, suppliers, and finance, they've enabled the WCK method to scale across the globe. These are all processes embodied in Declare It Center.

I expect their impact to be greater in the years to come, much like the impact that Jane Jacobs had in influencing our understanding of cities as complex problems, and the impact that teams helping fix Healthcare.gov had on our understanding of building human-centered software as a complex system, WCK is one of the organizations reshaping our understanding of disaster response as a complex opportunity to engage local communities in shaping their own solutions.

These case studies illustrate many of the Declare It Center processes, but it is not intended to be a complete list. Chapters 5 and 6 describe others, both in case studies and in detailed playbooks from Truss. Your teams and organizations will have your own processes, unique to your circumstances and constraints.

The core message is that in order to capture the value of your experiments and innovations in solving complex problems, commit to building Declare It Center processes to systematize, scale, share, and sustain your work. You've read about several ways to Move to the Edge and Declare It Center. The case studies and examples illustrate the Exterior practices – those you can share with your team that result in tangible artifacts like retrospectives. At a psychological level, when we build infrastructure, we are tapping into Kahneman's observations about the Fast and Slow Brain.[23] Creating repeatable processes engages the habitual, automated "fast" brain, which means less effort and less burnout for you and your teams.

But speaking of psychology, there's one more part. All the frameworks in the world won't work if you haven't been practicing for moments of uncertainty, the discomfort of being under stress, or the difficult choices when the right answer isn't written in a management book. The challenge awaiting you as a leader – whether you lead a team, a movement, a nonprofit, or a company – is to prepare for those moments in advance. We can train for these challenges by looking inward and developing Interior practices.

The next chapter is about *us*.

Chapter 4

INTERIOR PRACTICES: GET COMFORTABLE WITH BEING UNCOMFORTABLE

> "How you gonna win, if you ain't right within?"
>
> —*Lauryn Hill*[1]

When I asked Jana, the fire-response volunteer profiled in Chapter 3, about what she had learned since 2017, she surprised me. "It was terrifying but empowering to be thrust in this situation. I never thought I was the kind of person that could do that. I mean . . . before volunteering, I wanted the highest-paying job with the least responsibility! Now, one of my key phrases is *being comfortable with being uncomfortable*, and then just kind of holding space for that and settling into how we can process the fear."

So far, I've described Move to the Edge, Declare It Center as a framework, focused on building mastery of craft. But a framework is empty without the inner work – the Interior practices – that focus on building mastery of self. In my experience, working toward mastery of self becomes even more important as leaders take on more responsibility and their decisions have larger consequences.

It's not an accident that NASA, sports teams, and Navy SEALS, among others, have researched and developed training programs for high-performing individuals confronting high-intensity, high-stakes situations. The research of Anders Ericsson shows the impact of deliberate practice, popularized (incorrectly) as the 10,000-hour rule.[2] Highly accomplished musicians and athletes focus on improving the most challenging parts of their repertoire.

The emotional and mental strength that emerges from deliberate practice transfers to making decisions under stress, uncertainty, and unknowns. In addition to Ericsson's research, I have my own 10,000 hours in the following areas: a lifetime of soccer culminating in winning an NCAA national championship, a 27-year meditation practice, starting and building Truss, and finally, the survival skills from being Black in America. Kicking a soccer ball doesn't help me assess the risk of starting a company, but experience of recognizing fear in my body, making very public mistakes, and most of all, thinking clearly under intense pressure have all made me a better leader under uncertainty. I'll share a short background on the area of my deepest expertise, before going into the Interior practices.

I started playing soccer at age six with the new East Fishkill Soccer Club started by my father and a group of first- and second-generation immigrants in the Hudson Valley of New York. I still remember watching training films of the 1970 Brazilian World Cup winning team, and thinking I was watching magic, music, and movement all in one. I had the fortune of dedicated parents, coaches, and teammates, and I learned how to raise money to compete in tournaments around the US, Canada, Scotland, and Germany before age 16. When I was accepted at Duke University, I knew I needed to step up my game because the Duke team was ranked #1 in the country.

I got used to being humbled in my frosh year, starting with noticing that I was not listed on the roster in the preseason brochure. I played intermittently in my first three years, always a substitute, but never breaking into the starting lineup. It was a test of my commitment and love for the game, because I was balancing the course load of a biomedical and electrical engineering major and I was expected to hold a high GPA as an A.B. Duke Scholar. It came to a head in the summer before senior year (and I write more about that in the *Purpose Playbook* section).

The biggest lessons came during my senior year. We lost our first match of the season, got blown out by University of Virginia 4–0 and UCLA 3–0, and had to win our last game against archrivals UNC 1–0 to barely qualify for a spot in the NCAA tournament. Not the typical pedigree of a championship team, but we were building something invisible to outsiders: our mental toughness.

That Duke team wasn't the most talented team in the country – our loss to UCLA made that clear. But we were the most physically fit team in the tournament. Starting with "two-a-days" in the heat of August in North Carolina, through the dread of seeing "No balls, bring flats" on the locker room door, we knew we were in peak condition before the NCAA tournament.[3]

During the NCAA tournament, an extraordinary thing happened. Everyone, from starters to players who didn't make the tournament team, pushed themselves to the edge during our fitness drills. All of us knew an essential truth – in the last 10 minutes of the match, when the body starts dragging, the mind follows. If you have a lapse of concentration on defense and forget to watch your opponent sneaking behind you, the next thing you know they've scored. Your team lost the match because of *your* mental mistake, and there's nowhere to hide.[4] Instead, we practiced for those lapses, doing concentration drills *after* we were tired, committing movement to muscle memory instead of relying on our thinking. By the time we started the NCAA tournament, not only were we confident that we could outsprint our opponents, but we also believed we were mentally tougher in the last 10 minutes than anyone in the country.

Six weeks later, we had to prove it at the highest stage, in the NCAA final against University of Akron. We scored the only goal early in the second half, and we took control of the flow of the game as time ticked down. Still, Akron had three corner kicks in the last 90 seconds, and any lapse in our concentration could have allowed them to tie the game. But our training, earned in the humidity of the North Carolina summer, kicked in. We held our concentration and celebrated winning Duke's first national championship not just in soccer, but in any sport.

I'm using my experience of soccer to illustrate some important Interior practices. I suspect you have your own 10,000 hours of deliberate practice in your history, and I imagine you can draw from those experiences as the emotional and mental training for *being in the arena*,[5] an apt metaphor for stepping up in times of uncertainty and complexity. I've grouped the Interior practices that have been most decisive in my experience, and the rest of the chapter will explore them in more detail:

- **Meditate/Mindful training:** Practice meditation and mindfulness to learn how to calm and clear your mind. This is training for making decisions under stress and uncertainty.

- **Learn from your body:** Learn what your body is telling you, often before your mind is consciously aware. This is training for stress and preventing your own neurochemistry from hijacking your best responses.

- **Find your purpose:** Learn what's at your center, as training for filtering what's most important to you, enabling better decisions when facing the unknown.

- **Imagine your outcome:** Learn how to get unstuck, especially when you have several great options. This is training for how to decide and move forward.

- **Practice, practice, practice:** Learn how to avoid burnout. This is endurance training, because your best work is a lifetime of effort.

While there is a sequence to these practices, you can focus on any one of them to develop the skill or return to the practices depending on the situation. There are *lots* of Interior practices, and this chapter isn't intended to be comprehensive for all of the options.[6] I couldn't even document all the ones that I've used, tossed, or adapted for myself! The key point, however, is that these are *practices* that help you train for the moment you need to make decisions under uncertainty, handle complex challenges, and be a better leader under stress.

Practice: Meditate/Mindful Training

I nodded a silent thank-you to my fellow cleanup crew, dried my hands, and walked into the bright Southern California afternoon. I tried to walk mindfully to a good spot to listen to the next dharma talk, while being aware that I was hurrying despite myself. After three days at this silent retreat at the Deer Park Monastery in 2014, I was excited to hear Thich Nhat Hahn speak again.

Early in the talk, he reflected how often people ask him a simple, direct question. How do you end suffering, Thay?[7] His answer:

In order to end suffering, you have to get good at suffering.

He let a few beats pass while we took that in. His lesson that day was that we will all encounter experiences that cause us hurt or pain. But our *response* to that hurt is often the source of unnecessary suffering. As we practice mindfulness, we can acknowledge that hurt without amplifying it, lashing out at others, or swallowing it to reside in our bodies.

Thich Nhat Hahn's lesson about getting good at suffering echoes Jana's reflection of getting comfortable with being uncomfortable after her years of doing emergency response. This is the first Interior practice: In order to make decisions under uncertainty, you have to get good at being uncertain.

Meditation and mindfulness practices have been an important part of my life for many years, but it wasn't always that way. I had a less-than-stellar introduction. I tried to learn how to meditate in 1988, attracted by the appeal of managing the stress of my first job as an associate consultant at Bain and Company in Boston. But I could never "do it right." I'd sit, and whether I repeated mantras, counted breaths, or stared at a candle, my mind jumped from the pain in my knee to "How much time is left?" to "Will my roommate come in and make fun of me?" I couldn't shake the notion that unless I was in a monastery or somehow enlightened, I'd never get it.

I gave up for a few years, until my friend, Matt Hammer, called me from Jackson, Mississippi, and told me about this monk that Martin Luther King Jr. recommended for a Nobel Peace Prize in 1967. That monk, Thich Nhat Hahn, created a nonviolent protest movement in his native Vietnam, using the precepts of meditation as active resistance alongside his community. Exiled in 1966, he settled in France, started Plum Village Retreat, and began publishing. I was excited about the backstory, but I still avoided meditating. Matt kept nudging for a year, until he gave me the book *The Miracle of Mindfulness* when we met up at the New Orleans Jazz Fest in 1993.[8] I read *The Miracle of Mindfulness* in the mornings before beignets, crawfish boils, and The Rebirth Brass Band.

I was more receptive to the ideas, in part because I knew Thich Nhat Hahn put his practice *into* practice. But the key moment was reading a passage that described the following. When you're doing the dishes, does the dish ever slip out of your hand, breaking in the sink? Do you wonder how that happened? You were probably talking on the phone, watching a show on television, or planning tomorrow's meeting in your head.

Wash the dishes to wash the dishes.

That phrase hit me over the head in wonder. Washing a dish *is a meditation.* I can give my full attention to washing a dish. I can wash the dish with gratitude, recalling all the meals it served, the hands that created the dish, and the raw earthen materials used to make the dish. I realized in that moment that meditation is a practice for anywhere, anytime, with everyday objects.

I started my practice on that day. I eventually learned to sit and breathe, did one, five, and eventually 10-day silent retreats. Among many things, I learned from many teachers that the mind does what it does – think, plan, worry – but that doesn't mean you're failing. It means, in this present moment, you are aware that you are thinking, planning, or worrying. This practice is powerful, because you can begin to become aware of your own reactions, especially under stress.

There are innumerable meditation and mindfulness practices rooted in different cultural, spiritual, and religious traditions. I was raised Baptist, and while Buddhist meditation is my primary practice now, the tones of hymns and prayers echo in my memory. You may have your own traditions to draw from, and the most important thing is to develop your practice.

There's ample research into the power of the highly aware, open, calm state of mind, from Flow states to "the almost trance-like state jazz artists enter during spontaneous improvisation."[9] Cultivating this power is a rich substrate for high performance. We can train for those moments with an intentional practice of stillness. The opportunities to practice are abundant, from taking two minutes to breathe before a speech, taking a walking meditation through a forest, or mindfully cutting back the weeds in the garden. Instead of hoping you are ready for that moment of uncertainty, you can train to get good at it.

"Welcome. Breathe. You are already here."

Loudspeaker greeting before the start of a full-day silent meditation, as we arrived, still rushing

---

Practice: Learn from Your Body

Moving to the edge with the body is training for moving to the edge with the mind. They are part of the same system. There is a large and growing body of research that shows this interconnection.[10] I suspect most of us aren't training to be an elite athlete, musician, servicemember or astronaut; however, we can practice moving to the edge with our bodies at any time.

I shared the experience of playing soccer at the edge of my physical limits, and how that proved to be decisive in maintaining our concentration during the NCAA championships. The following story is from a different physical challenge that taught me a technique I use at work as well.

Climbing Mont Ventoux

"High knees. Drop shoulders. Slow breath. Next spot of sun."
—*My two-hour "meditation" mantra while cycling the Tour de France route up Mont Ventoux*

I rounded the curve and looked up through my smudged goggles at the mottled, shaded incline in front of me. This is the famous part of the route. This is where cycling legends are made. The section that I used to watch at 5 a.m., listening to the commenters Phil Liggett and Paul Sherwin marking who was breaking off the back of the peloton or accelerating to put their rivals in the red. I was at the 11 percent grade on the Tour de France route of Mont Ventoux, one of the legendary climbs of professional cycling. And I was scared.

I needed a vacation after being laid off from Linden Lab in 2009. I like traveling to non-English-speaking countries when I am between jobs or after a big project, in order to scramble my brain and jolt me out of my habits. I hadn't visited southern France before, late May was warm and before the main tourist season, and rumor has it they know a little bit about wine in Provence and the southern Rhone. I booked a small cottage in the village of Mormoiron, and then realized that it was only six miles from Mont Ventoux.

I was cycling, but I wasn't *training*, and with only three weeks in between, I didn't have enough time to be in peak condition. Then again, I reckoned I might never have the opportunity again, and I'd regret not attempting the climb, so I rented a bike near the mountain. I questioned my judgment when I drove up from Nice and saw this giant, intimidating bald hunk of rock from the highway, and imagined the suffering I was about to experience.

Professional riders have died climbing Mont Ventoux. There is a memorial to Tom Simpson, who died in 1967 during that stage of the Tour de France, in the bald rocky section near the summit of the mountain. The route is an unrelenting climb of 1610 m (5282 feet) in 21.5 km (13.3 miles) from Bedoin, with no real switchbacks where a rider can get a brief rest. Though the average incline is 7.7 percent, the middle section is the steepest. Because of the fame and the challenge, there are abundant resources about how to climb it, from detailed maps to specific tactics.

Basically, there are three sections. The lower climb is "easy" at 5 percent grade for 6 km. The middle section is brutal, turning under the forest canopy at an average 9 percent grade for 10 km. The final section of Ventoux (French for windy), above the tree line and into the bald, windswept moonscape summit, is a merciful 7 percent grade for 6 km. I studied the maps to get mileage markers, then looked at footage from old Tours to get visual markers. It provided some comfort to know what to expect, and I did

(continued)

whatever training I could to prepare for the moment on the edge.

From the start of my ride, my key focus was to preserve my energy. I didn't need to go fast. No one was looking. My goal was to get to the top. So for two hours I repeated the mantra in my head, "Drop your shoulders, Lift your knee, Slow your breath." After 45 minutes, it dawned on me that I was using the same practices as yoga and meditation. Stay in the moment, focus on the breath, calm my body. Cool! Training in one discipline is applying to another!

I knew exactly what was coming when I came around that curve. I had memorized the mile mark, the curve, and the long, straight incline ahead. If I could get to the top of that straightaway, I knew the worst was over. But then my default brain started to panic. As I felt the grade get steeper and my pedals slow down, the panic voice wanted me to stop, take a breath, assess my energy, eat a bar, check my water, survey how much further, and a hundred other distractions. Except, I was certain that if I stopped, at that gradient, I'd lose all my momentum to continue and I'd have to turn around in failure.

I focused on a patch of grass about 10 m in front of me, and said to myself, "I just want to reach that blade of grass." When I hit that blade of grass, I focused on a patch of sunlit road, and said, "I just want to reach that sun." I spotted a patch of oil, a leaf, a fallen limb, each successively 10 m ahead. I didn't plan this, and you can probably tell that I was moving so slowly that these markers were easy to spot. I was at the edge of quitting, and this practice was the only way I could quiet my panicking mind.

There was a pause, and then the grade increased again and I snapped back into finding the next leaf, grass, or spot of sun. After a few moments . . . or was it minutes . . . I stopped seeking the leaf and I was in the flow of the moment. The flow wasn't blissful and expansive – I was still right on the edge. But my mind was quiet and I was simply turning the pedals. The next thing I knew, I hit the top of the incline, the gradient declined to 7 percent, and I knew I'd finished the hardest part of the test. When I reached the top, the other riders and tourists clapped me in. I learned it's part of the tradition to applaud everyone, no matter how slow, who finishes the climb up that mountain. I took a photo, clapped in the other riders for 30 minutes and then did a fast descent back to Bedoin.

The mountain showed me how I could learn from the stress on my body and train my mind to overcome major uncertainty and fear. At the crucial moment when I wanted to flee – back to those stress reactions in the Introduction – I recalled my Interior practices of meditation and yoga. When I had the big moment of uncertainty, at the 11 percent grade, I broke the big problem into small, repeatable components, and was able to overcome the biggest challenge.

Without realizing it, I had unlocked an approach to a difficult pattern in my professional life. When I start a big project, I can get overwhelmed by all the stages of work necessary to get to the outcome I want. I think about all the complexities, the challenges, and the energy required . . . and become mentally paralyzed for days. Even while writing this book, despite *knowing* how to iterate, I watched my mind splinter into a thousand competing thoughts more often than I'd like to admit.

(*continued*)

But when I recall, "Drop shoulders, slow breath, next spot of sun," something in my body engages the lesson from Mont Ventoux in ways my mind cannot. I get out of my chair, go for a walk, get on my exercise bike, or do a short workout. When I intervene before I feel overwhelmed, it's easier upon my return to pick one task, get it done, and move on to the next. I've done a lot of *high knees, drop shoulders, slow breath, next spot of sun* while writing this book!

Steve Kerr, coach of the NBA Golden State Warriors basketball team, and Pete Carroll, coach of the Seattle Seahawks football team, say that competing is about vulnerability.[11] In my mind, that includes competing with my own beliefs. The moment at 11 percent was obviously vulnerable, but so was the choice to go up the mountain, or to write this book. This is why the Interior practices are so important. The road, the maps, the training, the bike, the shoes are the Exterior practices – akin to the methods and processes of Move to the Edge, Declare It Center. But those couldn't get me up the mountain without the training in the Interior practices, like meditation, vulnerability, and gratitude.

To close this section on learning from the body, some wisdom from a Greek philosopher.

From my experience when I think, "Oh yeah, I did this . . . I'm so great. I had 25-10-10," or whatever the case might be because you're gonna think about that.[12] Usually the next day you're gonna suck. Simple as that . . . [in] the next few days, you're gonna be terrible. I figure out . . . a mindset to have that like when you focus on the past, that's your ego: "I did this, we were able to beat this team."

When I focus in the future, it's my pride, like, "Yeah, next game is game five. I do this and I'm gonna dominate." I focus in the moment, the present. That's humility, that's being humble. That's saying no expectation. That's going out there enjoying the game, competing at the high level. . . . That's a skill that I've tried to . . . master, and it's been working so far. Yeah, so I'm not going to stop.

—Giannis Antetokounmpo, center for the NBA Milwaukee Bucks, speaking at press conference in July 2021 during the NBA Finals. Giannis scored 50 in the title-winning final game)

Practice: Find Your Purpose

Under the lights on an October night in 1985, Duke University's assistant soccer coach read the names of all the players who would be named to the 18-man NCAA playoff roster. He skipped "Harper." I don't recall breathing as I walked off the field, staring at the grass to avoid deepening my humiliation by catching the eyes of my teammates. That following weekend, we lost in the first round. I wouldn't have been a difference-maker, and it was painful to watch some of my teammates end their careers in a game we all loved. I woke up the next morning considering whether I should end my soccer career as well.

The next summer, I stayed in Durham to take organic chemistry, take the MCAT premed exams, and work in a lab to deepen my biomedical engineering major. In July, after a solo pre-season training run in the North Carolina heat, I decided to quit soccer. I was done with the endless training, the demands on my time, and I thought it would be nice to have a "normal" senior year.

It lasted about two weeks. My single motivation? I wanted to earn my letter jacket, a single artifact to show my kids someday that I was once a Duke varsity athlete. My exploration of quitting – an experiment, looking back on it – renewed my connection to my purpose, my love of *o jogo bonito*, the beautiful game that I had played since age six. I returned to training and entered senior year renewed and relaxed.

That was one of my first experiences with intentional, deliberate declaration of purpose. Over the years, with many iterations, I was able to develop the *Purpose Playbook*. We'll go through the *Purpose Playbook* in detail because it's a fundamental way of thinking that can guide leaders to anchor their own purpose and filter multiple opportunities. It can help you make better decisions – even when you don't know the answer, you can be guided by your purpose.

The turn of the year is a time for reflection, and for many people the output is a list of Resolutions.[13] While the impulse is strong, the failure rate is high. According to Statistic Brain, 42 percent drop their resolutions within a month.[14]

The instinct to start a new practice at the beginning of the year has research behind it. Professor Katy Millman coined "the Fresh Start Effect" to reflect her research that when there is a start to something new – a job, a Monday, a house, or year – it triggers a temporary lift in optimism. The sense that "I can be better" triggers a belief in the possibility of change. Her research suggests that the temporary suspension of pessimism is necessary to take the required actions to change into a "better self." The key is to take at least one concrete action that catalyzes the change you are trying to seek. That's the signal for Declare It Center, a piece of infrastructure that enables you to take an insight and turn it into a repeatable process that reduces the overall effort to achieve your outcome.

If you start the *Purpose Playbook* at the beginning of the year, you can take advantage of the Fresh Start effect. However, that's not a requirement – start on a Friday night and finish on a Monday! If you're reading this book, you already have the desire for something fresh, so let's get started.

The detailed playbook is below, but in summary, there are four steps: Review, Write, Publish, and Check-in. The playbook is based on practice, research, and lots of revisions. Here's what I've learned so far:

- **Purpose, not resolutions.** Purpose animates great companies, social movements, and personal change. For me, purpose is more powerful than resolutions because it aligns action when situations change, or when opportunities arise. *Forbes* contributor and author Mei Fox's article helped me define purpose,[15] and her catalog of interviews with leaders on purpose is a great resource.[16]

- **Practices, not goals.** Practice generates the focus required for significant change and sustained power. This is echoed in diverse sources from Buddhist monk Thich Nhat Hahn, research on habit formation from James Clear,[17] and brain science research cataloged by Ellen Leanse in the *Happiness Hack*.[18] Goals are motivational, but the practice gets you up in the morning.

- **Ship and iterate.** The best engineers and designers I know focus on prototyping, testing with customers, shipping, and iterating from feedback. Rather than writing "perfect" resolutions, I send a draft to friends and colleagues, get feedback, then review quarterly to improve clarity and focus.

Exercise: The *Purpose Playbook*

You've read the rationale; now it's time to get started with the playbook!

Review (3–5 hours)   I break this up over a few days.

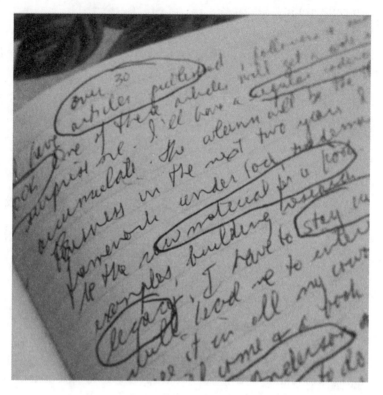

Here are my notes for the "By the end of the year" exercise:

- **Survey the past year.** This part is fun. Open your calendar, photo library, work notebooks, or project trackers for the past year. Grab your favorite relaxation beverage, start at January, and write freehand notes for each month about people, places, events, feelings, wins, and regrets. Don't evaluate, edit, or organize at this stage.
  - **Calendar:** Scheduled time = priorities. I always find something that surprises me.
  - **Photos:** Public and private photos reveal different priorities than the calendar.

- **Journal/work notebook:** Writing can reveal themes that aren't recorded elsewhere.
  - **Project trackers/Key meeting notes:** Do you remember what you were working on 12 months ago? I don't. Remembering what I (and my teams) actually did is embarrassing, humbling, and gratifying.

- **Imagine the upcoming year.** Write for 30 minutes, stream of consciousness, no editing, about what the next year will be. "In December 20XX, I will look back and . . . ." is a good prompt. I write about all the senses: morning quiet before a big presentation, aromas in my kitchen, muscle fatigue after a century ride. This technique engages my whole brain and body, an important source of knowledge as we explored the Interior practices exercises in Chapter 6.

- **Evaluate past-year purpose vs. reality.** This can be a humbling experience, but as my cofounder Mark Ferlatte says, if you achieve all your goals, you weren't reaching far enough.

- **Write past-year keys to success.** I record what behaviors, actions, choices, people, and influences drove my successes. I want to prioritize the "keep doing" list over the "stop doing" list – for now.

- **Review (or write) 3- and 5-year milestones.** Not everything can be accomplished in 12 months! This helps keep short-term priorities aligned with the long-term vision.

- **BREAK!!** After this stage is done, I stop for at least a day, letting all the reflections and evaluations macerate in my brain. The brain uses the extra "space" to make connections and reprioritize concepts without conscious effort.

Write (2 hours to draft, 3 hours to edit)   First draft of Upcoming Year: Do each of these steps in 30-minute increments, with a short break in between. No editing yet.

1. **Values:** Guidelines for action, written in short, memorable phrases that help you make trade-offs. Include quotes and images as well.

2. **Milestones:** Identify specific, concrete, measurable markers. These should be largely under your control.

3. **Key practices:** Measurable, repeated actions that support achieving milestones. Focus on only one per month.

4. **Purpose:** Write a phrase that is the driving force for the year. I often do this last.

    Do a reality check. Editing is the key activity. It requires a ruthless red pen and useful constraints. My favorite constraints are:

1. **Essential:** Only keep items that you would rate 9 or 10 in importance, on a scale of 1–10. Taking a practice from Essentialism, even the 8s must go.[19]

2. **Calendar:** One new habit per month, one major milestone per quarter.

3. **Timebox:** You only have 168 hours/week. Subtract sleep, work, eating, childcare, etc. and there's less time than you might think.

    Second Draft: Add your influences. These might be podcasts, quotes, books, authors, friends, or art. This is a great practice to reveal context and your evolution over time.

Revise 3- and 5-year milestones. Are your long-term milestones represented in the upcoming year's actions? Or do you need to revise or remove a milestone or two?

Publish (1 hour)   **Make it visual.** Publishing goals in a visual, memorable, accessible format is critical. I create in Keynote and export to PDF so I can have it in my phone, desktop, or printed.

Share with friends. Send the second draft to at least two other people. Ask them to review it, give critiques and ideas, and keep you accountable through the year. In my experience, people are excited and often adopt the practice themselves.

Final edits. Congratulations!

Check-In   Periodic check-ins are the key Declare It Center practice to keep aligned and sustain effort during the year. For example, sometimes my core purpose is more clear on March 31 than January 1, so I'll update it having the benefit of 90 days of living with it. A few check-in practices:

- **Daily:** Author and coach Mei Fox showed me this practice.[20] Make three categories:
- **Grateful:** Write at least three things you're grateful for in the last 24 hours. *Tip:* When I'm stuck on a hard day, I do a quick scan of whatever is around me in that moment. Usually, there are wonderful things right in front of me – a hummingbird, a drawing my daughter made me, or the fog burning off – and I'm reminded to be grateful for those simple, everyday experiences.
- **Themes / Values:** Yes, I rewrite them daily. The repetition helps embed them in my Fast and Habitual Brain. As a

result, it influences my choices, especially during chaotic or uncertain weeks.

- **Done:** Write at least three things you did in the last 24 hours. Prioritize those that reinforce your themes or are progress to your goals. Over time, it is a reminder of the small steps you took to make progress toward big accomplishments.

- **Quarterly:** I review the entire document, crossing off completed milestones. The biggest value, however, is adjusting based on new information and context.

Done!

The entire *Purpose Playbook* is an Interior practice that helps you develop, clarify, and refine your anchors for making decisions. Investing a weekend to reflect on the past year and imagine the future can be valuable and fun, even when the year is hard. If you are like me, you will remember challenges you overcame, great decisions you made, and the occasional cringeworthy action that you'll never repeat. They are all opportunities to get 1 percent better next year.

The second value of this practice is that your purpose and intentions don't have to be perfect before you get started. Situations can change quickly – remember how many of our January 2020 goals we had to throw out the window within 90 days because of COVID? The *Purpose Playbook* is not about having the right answer; it is about starting somewhere and allowing the quarterly check-ins to help you iterate based on new information.

Finally, the daily, 10-minute repetition of Grateful, Themes, Done will help you make decisions, especially when things get complex or when you feel uncertain. When I get stuck or confused, using my three themes as filters often makes the decision a lot clearer.[21] It will keep you accountable to yourself, by making a habit of recentering on your most important values. Bonus: Do the *Purpose Playbook* with an accountability partner, meet quarterly, and remind each other of your commitments and celebrate your progress.

Practice: Imagine Your Outcome

Have you ever been stuck making a decision, especially between two great choices – or two bad ones? When the decision is between two great restaurants, or which long line to take at airport security, the consequences for the wrong choice are relatively small, like an arched eyebrow – "I told you so" – from a family member. But when the consequences are large, personally or professionally, feeling stuck can amplify anxiety and make it even harder to decide.

The previous Interior practices – meditation, learning from the body, uncovering purpose – are training to help you make better decisions under uncertainty, stress, and complexity. But sometimes you still get stuck. You've done all the analysis, sought advice from diverse perspectives, assessed risks and rewards, and taken a long walk to clear your mind – but the best path forward still isn't clear.

Time to use counterfactuals! In Chapter 2, I detailed a counterfactual called a premortem as an Exterior Move to the Edge practice for a team or organization. Counterfactuals are a way to imagine a specific future based on a decision that you are making today, then working backward from that future state to test whether that decision is the best one. For teams, premortems identify hidden risks or problems. For individuals, counterfactuals are a way to "try on" a decision – like which shoes to wear – and project how it will look and feel in the future. The specific counterfactual I've used many times is to Write a Letter to Yourself, and it came from a brilliant suggestion from a friend when I was struggling with a hard decision.

In March 1996, I stood in the atrium of the Littlefield Center at Stanford University, talking with my fellow applicants to the organizational behavior PhD program of the Graduate School of Business. It was the last of my five visits to different schools, and because schools tend to cluster interviews, a dozen of us got to know each other as we crisscrossed the country.

My two finalists were University of Michigan and Stanford. Both had great track records for launching academic careers, enabling students to publish with established professors, and good communities of fellow PhD candidates. I could follow my interests in how diversity influences small group behavior, how it creates both better outcomes and greater conflict within teams.[22]

Over the previous nine months, I had done my homework. I had researched professors' theoretical interests, interviewed recent graduates, and exchanged anecdotes with the network of fellow applicants across schools. I rewrote my applications dozens of times. At the same time, I was highly motivated to make a direct impact on organizations, and I wondered whether being a full-time academic would isolate me from that goal.

I was highly aware that I was a beginner. All my research reduced the risk of making a bad decision, but it wouldn't erase that I was about to make a life-changing decision. In other words, I was at my edge. I walked out into the bright spring Palo Alto sky, unspooling my conflict to a fellow applicant. She stopped me at the crosswalk, and said, "You need to write a letter to yourself."

Do you have a decision you are trying to make, but you're stuck? Try the following exercise – practice on a small decision first and see how it works for you before trying it on a big decision.

Exercise: Write a Letter to Yourself

Here are the steps I used in writing a letter, illustrated by how I thought about my decision to go to Stanford or Michigan:

First, identify your choices. It is important that your choices are distinct and independent, in order to evoke the feeling of closing the door on the other option. When the choices are muddy or mixed, I've noticed it indicates that I'm holding onto something that isn't fully articulated. For me, my choices were Stanford, Michigan, or opt out of academia.

Second, pick your highest-rated choice. It doesn't have to be a perfect choice, nor must you be 100 percent confident. (Otherwise, you wouldn't be stuck!) Choose your highest-rated option, based on your current knowledge. I chose Stanford to start.

Third, write a vivid story of your future life. Generally, choose between 6 and 12 months into the future. If there is an important milestone, pick a point just before or just after. Elaborate on how you spend your day, whom you interact with, what your home, office, or classroom look like. Capture the highlights as well as the daily mundane details. Record how you feel in each of these scenarios, including any negative or challenging feelings. You don't have to write a novel, but you should include more description than a series of bullet points. In my version, I wrote about prepping for my qualifying exams under sunny skies, visiting old friends in San Francisco, feeling happy about going deep into research, and feeling confident about being a future professor.

What you might notice at any time during these steps are feelings of resistance, second-guessing, or even grief. Perhaps you will feel excited, centered, or resolved. Great! All of these feelings are instructive but keep going at least through Step 3 without changing your choice. Then sleep on it. Those feelings might be your early warning system, or at minimum a signal that identifies risks of your choice that you can mitigate.

Fourth, "send the letter." Print your letter, put it in an envelope, address it to yourself with "Do not open until" the date that you picked. Put it somewhere you can find – I nearly lost mine in my move across the country! As much as I don't like paper, I found that the action of printing, addressing, and placing the envelope solidified my decision in a way that a digital file did not.

Last, open your letter! (at the right time). As you read in my own story, that final check can be decisive, but at minimum it will be illuminating. Independent of whether you made the "right" decision, you can learn how accurately you project into the future, recognize the cognitive bias in your logic, or clarify where you were most insightful. Reviewing your own decision-making is an incredible tool for where you need to train your intuition against your own biases or where you can "trust your gut."

So . . . what did I decide? What I learned was that Stanford was the best choice for me, yet I had reservations about the long road to becoming tenured. Using my letter, I could fully commit to my course of study, and then review how I felt before I took my qualifying exams. I left my home in Durham, North Carolina, sold most of my belongings, and drove across the country to start a new life on the West Coast.

My letter to myself has an epilogue. I went deep on the original papers of Professors Daniel Kahneman, Amos Tversky, and Mark Granovetter under the warm sun and palm trees, was mentored by Professors Maggie Neale and Charles O'Reilly, and found a community of fellow students, especially the late Professor Kathy Williams and Professor Damon Philips. But when I opened my letter 9 months later, I saw a problem. I was 95 percent confident in becoming a professor, but that missing 5 percent was the fuel I'd need for the next 12 years to become tenured professor. I decided to leave the program and apply to the MBA program instead. The letter helped me commit to my decision, *and* it gave me a mechanism to evaluate my decision at a later time. Without it, I would have continued to plug away in a career that would have eventually depleted me, regardless of whether I was "successful."

The letter to myself is a simple and useful Interior practice. After moving to the edge of my knowledge, I queried a diverse network of knowledgeable colleagues and used my interviews as experiments to test different solutions. Despite that, I had three great options, and I needed to make a concrete decision. The letter to myself was a structure to help me make a decision, commit to moving forward, and validate my rationale at a critical point in the future.

Practice: Practice, Practice, Practice

To close the chapter on Interior practices, let's walk through how to apply them when faced with an uncertain or complex situation.

- If you notice that your body is clenched, nauseous, or on alert, go back to learning from your body. Identify where you're feeling it, and give it a name.

- If circumstances have you feeling anxious and your mind is racing, go back to meditating. Count your breaths, or do a walking meditation around your block.

- If you're stuck between decisions, try a counterfactual like a personal premortem or writing yourself a letter.

- If you are trying to evaluate and decide between multiple options, go back to your Purpose Playbook.

You can use this framework at any level, or in sequence, depending on what you're looking for. But the most important part of Interior practices is the word *practice*.

With repeated practice, you'll develop your own method and refine your own skills, either by yourself or with coaches and mentors. Over time, you will develop more confidence in your training, so that when faced with unknowns and uncertainty, you can call on the right tools to make a good decision. Whether you are on the edge of your knowledge or helping people follow you, training with Interior practices will enable you to use the Move to the Edge, Declare It Center framework with skill.

If you want to step up for your moment in the arena, train for it in advance. Interior practices are training for being comfortable with the discomfort of that moment. Based on the testimony of high-performance athletes, artists, and first responders, those intense moments of uncertainty can conversely put them in a state of flow. There's no report of anxiety – often when people are in flow state, they don't report experiencing emotions at all.[23] The Exterior practices help you lead others toward the What, and the Interior practice is training Who will lead. (You!)

Intermission

THE NEW NORMAL IS COMPLEX. TRAIN FOR IT

> "I stood at the border, stood at the edge and claimed it as central. l claimed it as central, and let the rest of the world move over to where I was."
>
> —*Toni Morrison*

I started *Move to the Edge, Declare It Center* noticing that the pandemic, forest fires, and racial injustice focused the world's attention on complex problems, and left many of us feeling uncertain about an unknown future. We're aware of how many of the systems we assumed were complicated – well-understood with a "right answer"– are actually complex. Many of us weren't trained or rewarded for responding to complex problems, where we start from the vulnerable position of "I don't know" and leading with curiosity and inquiry.

The Move to the Edge, Declare It Center framework is designed to help leaders navigate the new normal of complexity and uncertainty. Because we are called upon to make decisions, the framework shares Move to the Edge methods to explore and discover potential new solutions. Declare It Center processes help leaders systematize, scale, share, and sustain the most promising solutions, enabling the others to follow and build on your work. These are the Exterior practices that you can use with your teams, organizations, or movements.

Spanning these Exterior practices are the Interior practices. Interior practices are training for leaders they use in advance, before they are inevitably called into the arena. In a new normal of uncertainty, getting comfortable with discomfort is a skill leaders can develop through practice, practice, and . . . practice.

Many of these insights are from research, and they also reflect my personal and professional experience of being in high-intensity environments. Whether it was winning a national championship, daring to make our salaries transparent, or writing a public letter about being a leader and a target after the killing of George Floyd, these practices have been tested over many iterations – and I expect they'll continue to develop in the coming years.

To conclude Part One, I want to share an experience that brought many of these practices into sharp relief, and then add a final piece to the puzzle – a call to action for all of us who accept the challenge of solving complex problems.

February 2012: Show Up, Speak Up: Getting the Call

"Everett, Dad's cancer is back again," my sister began. "They thought they got it out when they removed his stomach, but the tumor is at the base of his esophagus, and it's inoperable."

Luckily, I had pulled into the parking lot outside the Rockridge BART station in Oakland. I was prepping for a difficult divorce mediation session . . . but now this? I could feel the heat rising in my face – I had known that the cancer could return, after his original diagnosis two years before. But surrounded by towers of unpacked boxes, trying to be accountable to my cofounders and to my brave five-year-old daughter, how was I going to deal with this?

"If you want to see Dad while he's still lucid, you need to come home now," my sister said with the firm, loving clarity that only a family member who is also a medical professional can deliver.

In January 2012, my brand-new company launched its first product, a mobile app to help manage your calendar. In the first four months of 2012, I was also hit with a succession of setbacks: I divorced, became a single co-parent to my daughter, and my NCAA soccer national championship ring was stolen from my new home.

Before getting on the plane to New York to see my family, I had to Skype Mark and Jen to tell them the news. I was nervous and embarrassed. Would I be the albatross for my cofounders, depleting attention and energy from the hard work of building a company? My nightmare was a chilling conversation where Mark and Jen said, "We want to renegotiate the terms of ownership if you're going to be a taking leave of absence."

I put on my big-boy britches and made the call. I told them the situation, and ended my rehearsed soliloquy with, "Depending on how it goes, I'll be back in the beginning of March." I don't recall much of a pause before they both jumped in. "Take your time. Stay as long as you need. We've got your back."

I remember the tingling feeling behind my eyes. It's a sign that I am deeply moved, and a warning that I might start to cry.[24] I distinctly remember my shoulders dropping while my cortisol-fueled heart kept leaping out of my chest. We talked through all the things: detail things, planning things, checklist things, but the *real* thing was that when I said, "I don't know," they replied, "We've got your back anyway."

Earlier in the book, I wrote that sometimes you choose to Move to the Edge, but in other times, the world *moves* you to the edge, whether you like it or not. I didn't plan to start a company while getting divorced, becoming a single parent, caring for a dying father, and having my Championship ring stolen from my home. Fortunately, I had some Interior practices I could draw upon. I was meditating regularly, exercising to keep in tune with my body, and I had my yearly intentions already written. When my sister called, I was completely clear about needing to return home – I remember feeling very still, despite facing an incredibly difficult divorce mediation.

My cofounders and I had developed our own Move to the Edge practices – hypotheses, experiments, testing, and iterating – that I detailed in Chapter 3 in going remote for the first 18 months of our existence. We had faith in our commitment to follow those practices, which meant it was easier to say, "I don't know," and have faith we could figure it out. Trust in our practices has paid off over and over in the decade since we started the company.

During the rest of the year, as I adjusted to my new life as a bootstrapping, single-dad entrepreneur, I relied on my Interior practices to make it through. There were bleak weeks when my goal was simple: Get my daughter to and from school, make sure she felt secure at bedtime, and keep breathing. I used 10-minute meditations almost every day to remind myself to breathe, especially when I was worried whether I had enough money to pay rent that month.

Advance practice matters when there is pressure to make good decisions under high complexity and uncertainty, especially when there are serious consequences for making poor decisions. The memories of that year make me grateful that I had already started some of those Interior and Exterior practices.

But I couldn't have done it alone. In addition to my cofounders, other friends and colleagues stepped in at crucial times to help.

I needed trusted partners, with complementary skills, high integrity, and the commitment to step up when the things got hard. This brings me to the concluding piece of the framework – finding your imaginal cells.

Finding Your Imaginal Cells

Imaginal cells are distinct cells within a caterpillar that contain the blueprints for creating a butterfly. At the same time, they are not required for the functioning of a caterpillar. In fact, imaginal cells are considered antigens by the caterpillar's other functioning cells. Despite being the key to the ultimate existential problem that the caterpillar must solve – how to reproduce – the imaginal cells are fighting for survival while the caterpillar munches away on leaves.

The imaginal cell cannot drive the creation of a butterfly on its own. It must find, link, and form a network with other imaginal cells before it is destroyed by the caterpillar's own cells. However, when enough of these imaginal cells have linked, these cells signal the internal structure of the caterpillar to find the underside of a leaf, anchor to it, and dissolve itself into goo. The imaginal cells, now in charge, direct the transformation of a jellied mass of cells into structures of legs, wings, eyes, and antennae. Once formed, the butterfly emerges, dries, and flies away, one step closer to the goal of surviving and reproducing.

I first heard this story in 2014 after I described to a friend how Truss and others helped fix Healthcare.gov. He remarked that while the journey from caterpillar to butterfly is a cliche, the mechanics are not – and they fit the experience of doing transformational change in organizations. I was so excited that I nearly named the company Imaginal.[25] I realized that searching for other imaginal cells mimics my experience of searching for others with similar blueprints to answer the question, "How do we build a company?" It also mimics the stories of innovation labs like Xerox Parc, and Kodak that generated blueprints for modern computing – the mouse, digital cameras, GUI – but whose organizations acted like the caterpillar, attacking these innovations with the antibodies of corporate bureaucracies.

It's the unfortunate pattern of organizational change, where new ideas meet resistance until there's a sufficient network of support – or they fail. When we work shoulder-to-shoulder with our clients at Truss, we also look for people outside of the daily project team who share similar mindsets and vision. They are our imaginal cells and linking with them is critical for completing a transformation project successfully.

The most striking part of this metaphor for me is that when the imaginal cells link, they don't simply reprogram the caterpillar to "grow" into a butterfly. They signal that it's time to dissolve into goo. It's not a neat or orderly process. Transformation is often a vulnerable, disordered mess. Knowing my cofounders had my back while my father was dying didn't make the next 12 months of building a self-funded company any more predictable, but it helped me focus on making daily progress toward our vision.

I think about the civil rights movement and how small imaginal cells in Montgomery and the Highlander Center linked to others around the country through organizing, boycotts, Freedom Rides, and marches. In earlier chapters, you read about Jane Jacobs and the Healthcare.gov team finding their imaginal cells to achieve historic victories whose influence is still manifesting.

Jana and Daniella both cite their imaginal cells, the network of professionals and volunteers, linked by common purpose and expertise, to make sense of an unprecedented situation. When I asked Daniella about how she maintained her energy in the pressure cooker of making public health decisions about COVID in the spring of 2020, she replied, "I have some really strong colleagues and people that reported to me. I really respect and trust their opinions and assessments, and that was the same of colleagues in our larger geographical region. It was so helpful to talk through these things, and we all supported each other in making some really hard decisions."

Fixing our climate is not going to happen just by moving to the edge with our brilliant ideas. It's going to be finding those imaginal cells in the form of a prime minister, a marine scientist, and a teenage climate activist, sharing their blueprints so we can start to build solutions. There is growing awareness that the problems of climate, homelessness, racism, inequality, artificial intelligence, and global poverty are complex. For example, institutional investors are pushing corporations to create measurable environmental, social, and governance (ESG) initiatives, or lose billions of investments.[26] The Business Roundtable declared that companies must maximize stakeholder (not shareholder) interests.[27] Organizations like CARE are updating their approaches to reducing poverty by focusing on gender-powered, locally led, globally scaled initiatives – a Move to the Edge, Declare It Center commitment that holds real promise. The Center for Applied Social Entrepreneurship at Duke's Fuqua School of Business is influencing the next generation of business leaders about creating systemic, scalable solutions that are distinctive among all top business schools. Bonus: For the generations coming of age today, the so-called *Gen Z*, these mindsets are the water they swim in – and just in time.[28]

If you are reading this book, you might be an imaginal cell. There are many others like you. You have a blueprint for the change you want to see. Since you can't avoid the goo, keep reaching for fellow imaginal cells, because once you find each other, your network is one of the systems to make your blueprints scalable and sustainable.

Ultimately, we need to show up and speak up in our moments of complexity and uncertainty. We need courage to be able to say, "I don't know, but I'm curious enough to find out anyway." We have the challenge, the opportunity, and frankly, the responsibility for solving these complex issues.

My call to action for you: If you want to lead your team, organization, or community in the twenty-first century, it's time to move to *your* edge and declare that your center.

Ring, Ring, Ring

In November 2018, I received an email titled "Time to Get the Band Back Together?" It didn't look like spam, so I opened it. It was an invitation to the North Carolina Soccer Hall of Fame ceremony in February 2019 in Winston-Salem, NC. The members of the Duke University NCAA Championship soccer team from 1986 were being inducted into the Hall of Fame.

Us. Me. "Hall of Famer"? Really?

In the Tacoma Dome, on December 13, 1986, after the final whistle, after the scoreboard read Duke 1, Akron 0, after the dogpile of all-blue bodies, after the lap of honor, after the trophy lifted high, what I remember most is how quiet the locker room was. We just sat in silence, chewing on sandwiches and grinning all over ourselves.

On the plane home, we met two Duke alumni, from 1939 and 1940. They told us they had been to every NCAA Final involving Duke since they graduated. A Rose Bowl in '39, Basketball finals in '63, '78, and '86, and a soccer final in '82. They'd finally seen Duke triumph after 50 years of trying.

That's when it really hit me – it wasn't just our friends, our parents, our classmates, who cared about our unglamorous, underfunded soccer team. There were thousands of alumni, prospective students, and soccer-playing kids who could claim a piece of Duke's first-ever national championship in any sport.

Each year since, I put on my ring for the two weeks around December 13, to remember our achievement and remind myself how much work, sacrifice, hurt, and luck went into that championship. I told myself that if it took me 14 years, from age 6 to age 20, to achieve something as indelible as a national championship, I could have the same persistence, resilience, and drive for a similar goal – whether it was raising a child or building my company.

When my ring was stolen from my home in 2012, it was literally the only object that could not be replaced. I looked into getting replicas, but since I was self-funding my company, I couldn't afford it while I was barely making rent. I decided to take the loss, be grateful that no one was hurt, and remember the lessons without the totem on my finger.

Now I was going to become a Hall of Famer, and as I made plans with my family to attend the ceremony, I thought about the missing band on my finger. My co-parent Julie Mikuta sent me an email one day, a usual occurrence in our week-on / week-off parenting schedule, but this one was different.

"What is your ring size? You need to go to the ceremony with a ring, and even though I'm a Hoya,[29] I want to get it for you." She had already made arrangements with Duke Head Coach and former teammate John Kerr to receive it at the sport office because it would barely be finished in time. And so, when I walked up to the podium with my teammates, I wore my Duke blue national championship ring.

Rings often represent a cycle, where the hope of renewal is within reach, even when the present moment seems uncertain. For Julie to give me a ring was more than the deep respect between former college athletes, former spouses, and current parents. It revealed, in a jolt of generosity and acceptance, how much our purpose to create a "new" family had outlasted the complexity and uncertainty of our divorce, my father's death, and the start of my company in those first few months of 2012.

There will always be uncertainty where we have to revisit our assumptions, open our curiosity, lead with questions, or admit "I don't know." There will always be forces that push us backward, into habits that no longer serve and beliefs that are no longer relevant. There will also be times of discovery, when the context of our lives changes, pushing us forward into the unknown. This book is the result of that curiosity and discovery, galvanized into action in the pandemic summer of 2020.

Part 2

PUTTING MOVE TO THE EDGE, DECLARE IT CENTER INTO PRACTICE

In this prescriptive part of the book, I use two examples addressing a similar complex problem to show the framework of Move to the Edge, Declare It Center in action. These examples will exhibit greater detail about how different Exterior and Interior practices are used by Truss and by West Paw to address diversity, equity, and inclusion (DEI), and show how using different tools at different stages helps generate sustainable systemic change.

Chapter 5

WHERE DO WE START?

"We're all White; where do we start?"

I hear this question all the time, especially after the murder of George Floyd in 2020 and the subsequent worldwide protests against racial injustice. Like many of my Black colleagues, I was flooded with requests, most well-intentioned and respectful but still exhausting to receive and to respond. In the months after, the question still lingers, and using the Move to the Edge, Declare It Center framework can help you sort through a sequence of actions that work for your organization or team. Here's the brief summary, followed by the case studies in detail.

First, start with your Interior practices. A commitment to DEI starts with you. Congratulations for taking it on – and prepare to be uncomfortable. You are almost guaranteed to say or do the wrong thing, over and over. You'll probably learn some uncomfortable truths about your community, your company, or you. Keep. Going. Anyway. Use some of the interior practices of meditation and mindfulness to be still with your discomfort.

For example, one of my old friends, a successful, highly educated White man, said, "I shouldn't have had to learn about the burning of Tulsa's Black Wall Street from a Netflix sci-fi show called *The Watchman*. I had no idea, and that's embarrassing." Start reading, discover your blind spots, and inhabit spaces where you are not the majority. Take a course in antiracism or Whiteness.[1] It will take years to unlearn and relearn, but keep making progress on sharpening your purpose, so it can guide your decisions. As Damien Hooper-Campbell, a senior executive and "human first" thought leader who built the inaugural DEI practices inside of Zoom, Uber and eBay, said, "Making progress on DEI is measured in *years*, not *a year*."

The following case study is a great example of how starting with Interior practices can anchor DEI initiatives.

Case Study: 2020: West Paw
Recruiting for DEI

"The realization that I had to do something – but not knowing what it was – came the week of George Floyd's murder," reflected Spencer Williams, CEO of West Paw. West Paw is a manufacturer of dog toys and dog products based in Bozeman, Montana. As a Certified B Corp, the company is eco-friendly in its manufacturing choices and people-centric in its business choices. With these values in mind, it's no surprise to me that Spencer was personally reflective about the events in the summer of 2020.[2]

"My first thought was, I don't have any context for what to do or what to say. However, I lived in Germany for a while, and I know that throughout history that silence is something that kills. I knew I could not be silent. I did a lot of reading and a lot of listening," he continued. "I'm certain I'm going to be wrong, but the first thing I did was reach out to my 70 employees."

He shut down the plant and invited everyone from all three shifts to join him on the outdoor patio, the safest place to gather during the pandemic. They formed a half-circle, and the team had a memorable conversation. Fueled by curiosity, Spencer asked how people felt about George Floyd, racism, and police violence. The team responded by sharing their own histories and experiences. While the employees of West Paw are diverse by age, family background, and professional specialty, they are also predominantly White. "I grew up in a house that was really racist. I felt embarrassed by it at school," shared one of the employees to heads nodding in recognition of their own history. Spencer could see that his employees were connecting emotionally on a deeper level and sensed how his choice to speak up was creating even greater community and psychological safety.

The team continued to speak up and speak out. West Paw sent a message to their customer and their retailers, that "we fundamentally support freedom and justice, that we will not remain silent, and this is what we must do to make change happen." Spencer added some insight about that communication. "I wasn't trying to be preachy. It was just straight to the point – this is part of our values."

This kind of vulnerable conversation happens when there is an established infrastructure of values, practices, relationships, and systems that engages every employee and invites them to act in alignment with those values. In other words, West Paw's story illustrates how the Exterior practices of Declare It Center (values) create space for the Interior practices (purpose) to emerge in a psychologically safe environment.

That was just the start of the journey for Spencer and West Paw. He and I met in the winter of 2021 as part of the Tugboat Institute, a network of Evergreen companies that are motivated to build purpose-driven organizations with positive long-term benefits to the employees, communities, and society.[3] I had just finished a virtual presentation on how Truss made our salaries transparent in order to further our value of diversity and inclusion, and he asked me a provocative question. He wanted to diversify West Paw's leadership team, but his company was located in Bozeman, where there are very few BIPOC residents, and his company was largely White. What advice did I have for him? I focused on three questions:

- Why did he, personally, want to hire a person to bring diversity to his company?

- How is diversity and inclusion connected to your core business model?

- Are you willing to invest in building networks of trust, not transaction, with BIPOC folks outside of Bozeman?

He told me the story of his reaction to George Floyd, and described the combination of personal and professional diversity his company needed in their next leadership hire. We discussed how investing in networks is a long-term strategy, and that leaders must prepare for awkward moments and being comfortable with the discomfort of being wrong – a lot. I was sharing the components of Move to the Edge to help him explore new networks, then Declare It Center by investing in those networks in order to build trust. Doing both would enable him and his company to navigate through the uncertainty, and make a great decision when they found the right person.

"I'll be honest; I didn't understand at first," Spencer reflected, "but I was really curious about how I could build these relationships in communities different than mine." Over the next six months, Spencer built relationships with BIPOC folks in multiple cities, and found a recruiter who was deeply embedded in communities of color. "It was a beautiful thing to see how we could diversify the skills of our leadership team and bring different insights with diverse backgrounds."

When I saw Spencer next in late June, he greeted me with enthusiasm and announced, "We have a new VP! He's excited to be moving to Bozeman with his family." After congratulating him and getting the details, I asked him whether there was any resistance within his organization. Spencer paused, and said, "Yeah, there's some challenges . . . ." My heart sank, anticipating the all-too-familiar story about "fit." But the story took a turn that I didn't expect.

Spencer got curious – a consistent mark of a leader who is comfortable with being uncomfortable. "The more I got curious, I realized it was less about them and more about me. I'm convinced that I have the right candidate and that we're going to have a few challenging conversations down the road. The reality is that this is a very different experience for most people here in

Bozeman. Some folks might need a little help getting there, and that's okay. I mean, that's what diversity is gonna bring."

Frankly, I was stunned.[4] His self-awareness was an example of the strength of his Interior practices for navigating a complex situation. When Spencer took a pause to reflect, rather than react, he was able to create a pathway for others to follow – the essence of Declare It Center.

While I love a happy ending, the power in Spencer's story is embodied in his decision to show up and speak up. His decisions were an apt response to the complexity of racial injustice and the uncertainty of "not knowing what to do." As a result, he has created the space for his entire company to build the psychological safety to Move to the Edge themselves. That moment on the patio when his company "talked story" will serve as lore to be told and retold as a part of West Paw's core values. While this story is about diversity and inclusion, it is really an expression of a new kind of leader and leadership that I hope to reflect in this book and inspire others to adopt for the coming decades.

DEI, Recruiting, and Hiring at Truss

Spencer's story at West Paw is a good example of starting with Interior practices (recognizing his own response to the George Floyd murder), creating a Move to the Edge moment for his company (gathering his company for a vulnerable conversation about race), and then using different Move to the Edge methods (reaching out to his imaginal cells) in order to successfully recruit a new leader who brings diversity of background and skills to West Paw.

At Truss, my cofounders Jennifer Leech, Mark Ferlatte, and I made a commitment, enshrined in our Truss Values, "to embrace diversity in people, voices, and ideas." In Chapter 3, you read about how that commitment manifested in making our salaries transparent, but that's only one aspect of a much deeper challenge. Bias in recruiting and hiring is a complex problem because it is enmeshed in a complex system of racism, sexism, ableism, homophobia, and a host of other biases.

Like other complex problems, there is not a silver bullet "right answer," but in this chapter you will get pragmatic advice and practice about how to think about recruiting and hiring, using Move to the Edge methods and Declare It Center processes. By the close, you will start to understand where to start, as well as specific ideas of how to adapt your current practices.

Start with Questions: More Inquiry, Less Certainty   As you read in Chapter 2, the first step is to start with questions. During the summer of 2020, when there were worldwide protests against racism, many other CEOs like Spencer, investors, and leaders reached out to me to get feedback on diversity and inclusion initiatives they were considering at their organizations. I usually responded by posing these questions, each of which linked to Exterior and Interior practices outlined in this book:

- Why is this important to YOU, personally?
- How does your personal "Why" translate to engaging your team or organization?
- Are you clear about the connection between improving DEI and your core business objectives, operations, or strategy?
- What is the outcome you are seeking?

The first question probes for *your* purpose, an Interior practice. Getting clear about this is important for leaders, because in order to overcome resistance and skepticism and gain trust, you will need the persuasive power of a clear purpose. Note, this does not mean that you have the answer – recall the story of John DiGioia starting a twenty-first-century university at Georgetown. He didn't know the answer, but he had a clear vision and a method for people to follow. You can use this same practice.

The second and third question probes your commitment to a Declare It Center Exterior process – are you willing to create the infrastructure and systems to make DEI a core part of the organization? One of the most common patterns of failure I've seen is when leaders skip that question. Instead, they will react, quickly allocating a small budget to a side project, usually in marketing, human resources, or to an ad hoc team. Without active executive sponsorship and a clear hypothesis of how DEI benefits the core of the business, these DEI teams are on borrowed time. As soon as there is a drop in sales, pressure on budgets, or a change in leadership, that side project is one of the first to get dropped. Not only that, that leader has damaged the trust with their current employees and potential recruits. You can avoid this outcome by going beyond DEI as "the right thing to do" and applying the same rigor that's required to build a new product.

The fourth question probes for a future vision, an Interior practice. Focusing on outcomes, not activities, will help your organization or team develop plans about how to achieve it. For example, our vision at Truss is that our employees reflect the diversity of the United States population. Once established, we worked backward to figure out interim milestones, like matching the diversity standards of our industry. You might notice this is a version of counterfactual that I wrote about in Chapter 3 (premortem) and in Chapter 4 (write yourself a letter), which helps you imagine a future state and then work backward.

In 2019, Truss contracted with Jen Tress and Abdul Smith of Verge Talent Partners to assess its talent acquisition and staffing function and create opportunities to strengthen it. In Move to the Edge fashion, the initial phase focused on discovery and delivering a set of findings and recommendations. Our team, led by COO Jen Leech, identified several outcomes:

- Visible hiring metrics that identify and focus improvement efforts
- Repeatable, effective interview processes for leadership roles
- Easy-to-use artifacts that support an effective hiring process (esp. job descriptions, work samples, interview guides, personas, and outreach channels)
- An excellent candidate experience
- The right makeup of hiring team resources to deliver on the above
- An understanding across Truss on how to staff for nonbillable roles

The methods used to identify opportunities included:

- Interviews with key stakeholders, including founders, directors, and the hiring team
- Review of all documents on the hiring drive
- Hands-on, direct management of operations

Interviewing key stakeholders, reviewing existing operations, and getting direct hiring experience are examples of Move to the Edge methods. They explicitly increase the diversity of viewpoints and are designed for blameless learning before we start the project. These methods are especially effective when there are fresh eyes on the system (a new employee or an outside consultant) because they can use their outside vantage point to question assumptions, ask new questions, and push the organization to develop new hypotheses. Our Salary Transparency project detailed in Chapter 2 started in much the same way.

Focus Area 1: Establish Hiring Goals and Metrics Dashboard to Drive Performance Truss can pull good data reports from Lever, our recruiting and hiring software, to get a sense of how long candidates are in the pipeline, the percent of candidates that convert between phases, and the diversity of the talent pool/hires we make. These data sets provide solid insights, but used alone, they don't drive performance in a consistent or predictable way. To do that, you'll want to set aspirational goals, and measure progress against them.

Recommendations:

1. Establish hiring goals, key performance indicators (KPIs), and targets.
2. Share internally with Trussels.
3. Report monthly at the all-hands meeting.

Aspirational goals set the target. Next, we use Move to the Edge methods, creating experiments and testing hypotheses to help us reach our goal. In contrast, measuring progress using software to communicate with transparency to the entire company is a Declare It Center process.

In addition, keeping a consistent cadence of communication with stakeholders is a critical Declare It Center process. This is an overlooked skill, and I find this to be one of the hardest things to get consistently right. This is even more difficult during a period of fast employee growth. With each new employee, the number of possible communication points increases exponentially. We always seemed to underestimate the amount of communication needed, and once we had anchored on the "right amount," we were behind again!

The next step was to decide which metrics to measure. They recommended metrics that are important to Truss, easy to measure (and thus report on), and commonly used by the private sector, as shown in Table 5.1.

TABLE 5.1 Truss Hiring Dashboard

Goal	KPI	Target / Formula	Analyze / Report
Attract and convert quality candidates.	Quality	35% of applicants in digital screen move to the intro interview phase (no target, but measure conversion) 3:1 interview to offer ratio	Candidate sources Conversion rates between hiring stages
Build a team that looks like the United States.	Diversity	Aligned with Census data for race / ethnicity, for example: 60% white, 18% Hispanic, 13% Black, 6% Asian, etc. and binary gender:[5] 51% female/49% male	EEOC categories Current levels & changes Diverse candidate sources Find sources of LGBTQI+ data, including reporting sensitivities
Deliver a predictable hiring process timeline.	Pre-planning Time to Hire	Planning phase of 10–20 days (20 for leadership) Meet time frame (for example, industry standard is 33–36 days*	Overall (aggregate) By practice By phase
Deliver an excellent candidate experience.	Candidate Experience	90% or above candidate satisfaction	Candidate survey results

*Lever 2019 Benchmarking the Industry Report, p. 38. Total median time to hire by company size (1–100 employees) for engineering, design and product management positions. Lever used anonymized metadata from its customer base. https://hire.lever.co/reports/benchmarks/talent-benchmarks-report-2019.

You may notice something about the benchmarks. We didn't use one singular benchmark to measure progress on a complex problem. There's ample data that optimizing on one single metric can lead to unintended results, because it usually underestimates complexity. My cofounder Mark reminds people, "We need a quality metric *and* a performance metric. Not only does multiple metric represent a diversity of perspective, but it also tends to represent key elements of a complex system, rather than a single interaction. This is how we use an essential property of complex problems—multiple elements with unpredictable interactions—and design a system to learn how to address it.

These Truss goals are aspirational. We know we're not there today, but we have a clear goal, and by being transparent, we can be honest about the journey it will take to get there. A common mistake – one we've made as well – is to establish a baseline, then expect it will be met immediately. It creates the condition for immediate negative assessment and blame-filled responses. Being up front, setting expectations, and reporting on results frequently – including failed experiments and mistakes – is the best way to reduce that skepticism and engage the doubters. Essentially, it's a parallel to the demo in agile development. Show, not tell, and do it often.

By frequently monitoring our final set of KPIs and targets, we can gain deep insight and engineer solutions that move us closer to our targets. Internally, it also demonstrates the company's commitment to these goals. All of these systems are Declare It Center processes because they put our Move to the Edge aspirations into daily, visible, repeatable actions that everyone in the company can follow.

Develop Hypotheses and Create Experiments   "I think one of the things that we've really appreciated about our time with Truss is that there has been a lot of room for experimentation," said Abdul Smith, cofounder of Verge Talent Partners. Over the years, we've done a LOT of experiments, from using targeted mailing lists, attending job conferences, and developing relationships with code academies and engineering schools. Most didn't deliver as expected, but we learned quickly because we had a clear idea of our outcomes and what results we wanted from any given experiment.

There's one thing to be aware of as you are developing experiments – you are *building relationships* with individuals, consultants, and companies as you pursue testing hypotheses. If your company is starting this journey, treat everyone as more than a transaction, and seek an exchange of value. The common experience of being a person who is both highly skilled and in an underrepresented group is that they are flooded by requests for their time, advice, and feedback. If you are reaching out to one of these folks, ask how you can support *their* efforts. Pay them for their expertise, and then show up and step up on their behalf. For example, sponsoring a DEI conference is good, but showing up in person, as a leader open and willing to learn, is a vivid, memorable, and distinctive act. Ultimately, these are your future imaginal cells, and I promise you that investing in building relationships will pay off.

Truss continues to develop hypotheses and run experiments. Here's one of our latest.

Focus Area 2: Reduce Time Candidates Spend in Pipeline   Our average pipeline speed (the time it takes to close a candidate) across all Truss jobs is higher than most companies, according to the Lever benchmarking data and the Society for Human

Resource Management, which reported a 36-day average time to hire in 2017.

We realized that work samples and final interviews accounted for the longest stages, delayed by calendar availability, work sample extensions, and a lack of alignment on artifacts and evaluation rubrics. Reducing the time in pipeline benefits everyone involved.

Recommendations:

1. **Time-box the planning phase (e.g., 10 days).** When a new role hits the open position sheet, the hiring team schedules a kick-off with the hiring manager and subject matter experts. In that session, we'll then . . .

2. **Validate artifacts needed, the level of effort, and who does the work.** Formally check in with hiring teams every six months to validate that current artifacts are attracting and converting a solid talent pool.

3. **Reposition work samples.** According to the 2019 Lever data, work samples account for the second-longest phase in the process, just behind final interviews. In theory, work samples are a good thing because they help assess a candidate's skills without unconsciously judging them based on appearance, gender, or age. But there is growing skepticism around the effectiveness of this method, and the burden it places on candidates.[6] Our newest experiment is to limit the assignment to less than two hours.

Here's where a Declare It Center infrastructure to build and measure each step in the process matters. We looked at our data. While we sped up the intake and screening of recruits, we overloaded the next phase of first interviews. All of a sudden, we had a bottleneck of candidates waiting for interviewers. Not only that, we shortcut our planning phase, so adjustments happened reactively and ad hoc instead of intentionally and in advance.

We also realized how many of our questions were subjective ("How do you feel about this person?"), which for us emerged as a bias for generosity. As a result, far more people passed to the next stage with subjective questions than with competency-based questions. When you multiply that effect by eight concurrent job postings, the result on the *entire* system is that you move at a glacial pace. Again, looking at the entire interviewing process as a complex system, then measuring the components of the system against our expectations, enabled us to correctly diagnose the problem. If we had focused on only one metric, or assumed a linear process, then we would have focused on the wrong thing (e.g., how fast are we getting applicants?), and wondered why we weren't getting the results we hoped for.

Instead, the insight was, how do we slow down, in order to speed up? This was the birth of the cohort model. Creating a cohort enables us to look at a group of folks, compare and curate them, and be intentional about creating a consistent experience.

In a cohort model, the hiring team gathers all the applications and does digital screens on a rolling basis. We then map the cohort against Equal Employment Opportunity Commission (EEOC) data to assess how diverse the candidate pool is, identify any trends in the candidates (e.g., we're getting too many overqualified people), and then assesses the entire cohort for the best candidates. Next, we address consistency. We make sure the interview questions are consistent, give directions to interviewers about how to make assessments, and then add forms to help guide and receive interview assessments.

Note: Even though the cohort model is a Move to the Edge experiment, we build tools and processes – like guidance forms for assessments – that enable anyone in the hiring process to use them with minimal effort.

Focus Area 3: Train the Recruitment Funnel to Deliver High-Quality, Diverse Applicants Compared to the rest of the software industry, Truss is doing pretty well in recruiting diverse employees. As of summer 2021, we had 53 percent she/her identified, 35 percent BIPOC, and 25 percent LGBTQI+ employees, and that is a direct result of our Move to the Edge experiments back in 2012, followed by our Declare It Center processes, systems, and infrastructure since then. Unfortunately, our pipeline is mostly reliant on active candidates – those who see the opportunity and decide they'll apply. We are likely missing out on a big passive candidate market. This is the next experiment we need to run to hit our aspirational goals.

Recommendations:

1. Invest in sourcing passive candidates. According to Lever, sourced candidates account for nearly a third of all hires.[7]

2. Continue to analyze channels to understand which attract top candidates.

3. Develop a structured, consistent interview process and rubric that focuses on probing for desired technical and behavioral competencies at all stages. This approach is also recommended by Project Include[8] as a way to reduce bias and increase fairness.

4. Create a diversity recruitment strategy that has multiple channels and touchpoints and is aligned to the roles.

In addition, we know that a subjective, inconsistent recruiting process is likely to introduce bias, and this has outsized impact on candidates whose backgrounds are underrepresented at the company. Ensuring consistency was a key process improvement in Focus Area 2.

Focus Area 4: Create a Great Candidate Experience   The quality of the candidate experience has an impact far beyond the candidates themselves. This particularly true when a company is recruiting candidates who bring diversity into the company. There are active professional networks for people who are underrepresented in different fields. News travels fast about companies that waste candidates' time or engage in a biased interview process. According to anecdotal feedback, Truss is doing well in this area, but creating measures for this is the next Declare It Center infrastructure we want to develop. It will help us stay focused and accountable, no matter who is on the hiring team.

Recommendations:

1. Assign a person or team to act as the candidate's guide throughout the Truss process.
2. Communicate interview steps and estimated timelines through email. Continually communicate with the candidate to keep them engaged. Provide updates if the timeline changes.
3. Create a candidate survey to identify what's working well and any pain points.

We communicate with candidates on a frequent basis, either giving them a polite decline or a congratulations, and always setting expectations for time and requirements. If we're not satisfied with the makeup of the cohort, we reopen the recruiting. If we are satisfied, we only send the top candidates to the next stage, where we can manage the flow with more intention and consistency, while speeding up the entire decision-making process for everyone – especially the candidates.

Concluding Words on DEI in Recruiting and Hiring   All four of these focus areas are important for DEI in recruiting and hiring. If you're thinking, "This is just a description of improving a hiring and recruiting system," you are absolutely correct. Declare It Center processes for DEI is about bringing Move to the Edge experiments – like a cohort model – into the core operational systems of the organization. When we have success with our experiments, we transform those experiments into the new normal.

Just like new habits seem awkward at first, but become normal with repeated practice, bringing your DEI experiments into your core recruiting and hiring systems means you can achieve your desired outcomes with less individual willpower. Putting a strategy together is key, but unfortunately, you can't predict the outcome. You need to continually talk through the process to see if these different mileposts along the way are delivering on your strategy.

I titled this chapter "Where Do We Start?" on purpose. While "How Do You Fix DEI?" would be an attractive title, that doesn't match the reality of addressing complex problems. Uncertainty is part of Move to the Edge, even when you do all the right things. In 2021, new complexities include the surge of Delta variant, companies experimenting with hybrid work, and an estimated 40 percent of workers who are considering resigning from their jobs. As Abdul reflected when considering DEI:

There's no silver-bullet answers here. I do think one of the primary challenges for hiring right now is the need to carefully consider the importance of having employees attached to a physical location. If you're trying to attract diverse candidates into places where BIPOC people don't tend to travel, or where local laws are hostile to health care for nonbinary people, those are big obstacles. People want to feel comfortable and safe in order to do their best work, and that's even more important after the challenging year we've had.

The DEI system work described above may not be as splashy as an emotionally moving ad campaign or a high-profile hire. However, using the practices and methods in Move to the Edge, Declare It Center, you will be clearer about your own purpose, prepared for the discomfort of "I don't know," and more concrete about your outcomes, and you will build initiatives that are right for you and your organization.

Slack Bot for Diversity?

Some of our most impactful Move to the Edge experiments with DEI came from our employees first. For example, when we were about 15 people, during one of our all-hands meetings, one of our women engineers held up her hand. She said, "You know, I'm noticing that when people address the entire group, they say, 'You guys.' Sometimes I do it too, but we should do better." Everyone leaned back in their chairs in a collective "Damn, she nailed it," gesture. Clearly, this habit was deeply ingrained, despite our elevated awareness and genuine desire to improve.

A few days later, one of our engineers sent a message to everyone. He had designed a Slack Bot.[9] Slack is our messaging service, and one of the features is that users can create automated responses, triggered by a keyword. His Slack Bot was trained to look for "you guys" and "guys" in texts, and write an automatic response. The responses were, "Did you mean y'all?" "Did you mean yinz?" "Did you mean peeps and non-marshmallow friends?" "Assembled guests?" "Sailors?" and so on. It was hilarious, clever, and highly effective.

The genius behind the experiment was that it gave immediate and direct feedback. It was transparent to the writer, but also to anyone else on the thread. No favorites. It "coached" toward a new behavior with a wink rather than a reprimand. Finally, because it is automated, it is a piece of infrastructure that is sustainable and scalable. The Slack Bot still works, the answers have multiplied, and most importantly, the use of "you guys" has dropped to nearly zero. Move to the Edge, Declare It Center can have a sense of humor, too.

Chapter 6

PUTTING PRACTICES INTO ACTION: SUSTAINING A REMOTE-FIRST COMPANY

Remote? Distributed? Hybrid? In-office? These questions are no longer theoretical, because since 2020 every company has needed to navigate this decision. This is a "live" complex problem that has affected everyone, and for those of you who are making difficult decisions about your companies, colleagues, and employees, I'm with you in experiencing many "I don't know" moments in the past two years.

There is no universal right answer, but I believe remote-first is the best answer for Truss, in part because we've put this hypothesis to the test for a decade. What's more important is that we used the Exterior and Interior practices in Move to the Edge, Declare It Center to come to this conclusion, and we remain open to continuing to improve and refine these practices so our employees and clients can thrive in this new normal of work.

This chapter concludes the book with the pragmatic nuts-and-bolts of how we build and sustain a distributed, remote-first company. The purpose of this section is to share the details of how we implement these practices at Truss so you can adapt them to your organization. In addition, there are some Interior practice exercises you can try on your own. Over the last decade, we've collected these practices into the Truss Distributed Playbook, so this is the result of many iterations, inputs, and experiments from the Trussels. It remains a work-in-progress, and I'm sure by the time this book is published, the Distributed Playbook will have evolved and be at least 1 percent better.

What remains, however, are two things. First, a commitment to Move to the Edge methods to navigate through the uncertainty and unknowns that will define the future of work in the coming decades. Second, the belief in Declare It Center processes to scale, share, and sustain the results of this work.

Exterior Practices

This next section details some of the Exterior practices we use to grow and sustain our distributed-first company. You will learn specifics about how we conduct these practices, as well as reinforce the concepts of Move to the Edge, Declare It Center in a pragmatic playbook.

I hope it will help you make the best possible decisions for your organization – even if you decide to be fully in-office. Not only can these practices support your employees to do their best work, but they may even help you interact more successfully with your clients and vendors. Writing this book in the first year of COVID and the Delta variant made me highly aware that this is a time of stress and uncertainty. I hope this guide, including the Interior practices, help you navigate these tricky waters – and perhaps emerge a stronger, more resilient company.

Using Hypotheses to Create Company Culture

The practices that would become Move to the Edge, Declare It Center sharpened in the formative stage of our business. We had beliefs and values, but we needed to test our thinking and get factual data. There are enough organizations that begin with a compelling vision but never test the underlying assumptions until they run out of grants, customers, or funding. I know because I've been at the end of the road of all three scenarios. I didn't recognize the pattern until I went to Founder Labs in 2011, learned the Lean Startup methods, and learned about building sustainable infrastructure from my Truss cofounders, Mark Ferlatte and Jen Leech, in 2012.

Even though we shared many of the same values about how to build – and not to build – a company, we recognized that we needed to test it. We wrote hypotheses, tests, expected outcomes, and risks, and documented when we were right, wrong, and what we learned. We used tools like the Business Model Canvas,[1] translated hypotheses into questions, then organized work in Pivotal Tracker to make it transparent. As we learned, we documented our decisions into playbooks, decision records, retrospectives, and the occasional hard-to-find-what-was-the-title document buried deep in someone's hard drive.

We needed to start hiring quickly, but in parallel we tested hypotheses about how we'd run our business. For example, we anchor on a 40-ish-hour workweek because we know that capacity for high-quality work decreases between 40 and 50 hours, especially for "knowledge work."[2] Our goal is expecting sustained great work, even under complex or intense conditions.

The outcome? Historically, we have low attrition, a reputation for a supportive work culture, and high performance on complex projects. Most of our business is a result of referrals, extensions, and expansions – the highest measure of client satisfaction. That said, our attrition rose in 2021. Like many companies experiencing the impact of millions of people reevaluating their relationship to work, we need to reevaluate our hypothesis about what creates a thriving work culture.

This decision has its own narrative of failed experiments, iterations, contrary discoveries, scaling challenges, and "*Duh*, why didn't we do that a year ago?" moments. At their core is a principle, a framework of Move to the Edge, Declare It Center, and a set of tools that manifest these decisions into the Truss culture. Let's examine in more detail the hypothesis to go remote first, and the tools, practices, and infrastructure we now use to keep our employees connected, effective, and thriving.

Deciding to Go Remote First

In 2011, the startup scene in Silicon Valley was accelerating. New startups clustered around South Park in San Francisco, accelerators like YCombinator and 500 Startups churned out dozens of startup teams, while angel investors and VCs spread money around trying to find teams that would transform into billion-dollar companies.[3]

The mix of money, fame, and power focused on seven square miles on the Pacific Ocean, creating its own culture, norms, symbols, and mythologies. One of them was the open office, filled with young men (and a few women) collaborating, inventing, disrupting, and creating the next big thing. Whether the office was in an apartment, warehouse, co-working space, or shiny new building, the ethos and energy of the open office became one of the influential markers of a modern company.

I worked in open offices most of my career, from Bain and Company in 1987, through Ninth House Network and Linden Lab in the 2000s. I've also worked at multi-office global corporations, where coordinating between time zones, locations, and languages was facilitated through phone calls, emails, or in-person visits. The quality of those experiences depended on connection, communication, and the space to do focused, deep work.[4] With the advent of better communication tools, the need to travel and commute became less acute, and the trade-offs between time spent in office and value created started to flip.

There is solid research and experience on the downsides of the open office.[5] Besides the interruptions and noise, open offices can be a cultural minefield for women, BIPOC, nonbinary, or neurodiverse people. For example, norms of productivity are often biased for visibility, cultural "fit," and extraversion. The COVID pandemic and experiments in hybrid work accelerated a reexamination of the core assumptions of what makes the best work environments.

For me, this is an opportunity to explore, experiment, and build systems to amplify what works – in other words, apply Move to the Edge, Declare It Center. Whether your company experiments with hybrid, distributed, remote, or in-office modes, keeping your employees connected to each other is one of the most important principles. Most of our work is now in teams, not individuals; therefore, our systems need to support those connections.[6] Our practice of distributed work focuses first on connection, then builds experiments and infrastructure around it.

Staying Connected

In Chapter 4, Daniella learned about the severity of COVID and developed a response policy because she stayed connected to her network of health-care professionals with H1N1 and SARS experience. Jane Jacobs's investment in staying connected to her neighbors (Chapter 2) enabled her to overcome one of the most powerful men of the twentieth century and preserve Greenwich Village.

We're all humans, even if we mostly only see each other in video chat. One concern of distributed teams is how to build connection and understanding when employees don't bump into each other in the hallway or by the proverbial water cooler. This concern became particularly salient when employees – who may not have had experience with remote work – were suddenly required to work from home because of COVID.

We wrote these practices about Staying Connected a few years before the COVID pandemic. Each of these practices emerged out of identifying an issue, proposing an experiment, learning, and iterating through feedback. Once we settled on a practice, we wrote up guidelines for others to follow and finally put it in a Truss Distributed Playbook.[7] In our experience, these practices help people stay connected, reduce isolation, and lift the energy of your team so they can keep doing great work. The following are some of the more important practices and methods that we use to maintain a remote-first company, divided into two sections: Staying Connected and Good Communication.

Being Humans Together (BHT)   One of the more creative and delightful ways to stay connected is to coordinate a standing video chat to talk about life outside of work. Being Humans Together (BHT) is an optional, half-hour weekly meeting at Truss, and many Trussels have claimed it's their favorite part of the week.

Here's how it works: Any team member who is interested joins the BHT video chat. If there are fewer than nine participants, each person gets two minutes to talk about anything they want to (talking about work is lightly discouraged). If there are more than nine participants, the meeting facilitator does a quick check-in to see how people are feeling, and then designates breakout groups of three to four people each; this allows participants to have more meaningful conversations. (We use Zoom for our videoconferencing software, which has a feature to randomly create breakout groups. For more information about Zoom, refer to the "Tooling" section.)

Sometimes, we have prompts for our BHT calls. Sample prompts include:

- What's one story about you that you think really represents what you're like?
- What's your favorite Dad joke?
- What's your favorite pizza topping?
- What's the story behind your name?
- What GIF are you today?

Have fun with it! The BHT call is a way to reflect and strengthen your own culture and values. Make a space for your team members to come up with a unique and creative expression that enhances the connections in your company.

Topic-Based Socializing   It's important for your employees to socialize in a lightly structured way, whether that socializing takes the form of working on craft projects, a book or movie club, or playing games together. Topic-based socializing allows your team members to build stronger connections, and it also fosters cross-team relationship building. It's a great way to prompt employees to learn things about each other.

To promote topic-based socializing, we create topic-specific groups in our messaging application. Employees can join as many (or as few) of these groups as they prefer. These groups allow people to discuss topics of importance to them, helping those team members form strong connections to one another. We've found that topic-based discussion channels really pick up once a company has more than 50 people. (*Note:* We use Slack as our messaging app. See the "Tooling" section for more information about Slack.)

Colleagues-and-Coffee Messaging Channel   A certain set of Truss employees are often able to make it to our BHT calls or participate in topic-based events, and some folks interact with each other often because they're on the same project or committee. To introduce some serendipity into the mix, we also have an opt-in channel that randomly pairs two (or three) Trussels together every other week. These Trussels hop on a short (30-minute) video call to discuss whatever's on their minds.

Our colleagues and coffee practice helps people to get to know other employees whom they might not otherwise interact with, fostering a greater sense of cross-team connectedness.

(*Note:* We use https://www.donut.ai to schedule the meetings and make the random assignments and Zoom to video-conference.) This practice is applicable to groups over 30 and is highly recommended for groups of 50 or more.

Celebrations Channel We have a bot to remind us of folks' birthdays and Trusselversaries (join dates). It also gets the gif party started. Team members opt in to have https://birthdaybot.io remind others of their birthdays or join dates in a stand-alone channel to keep distractions contained.

This practice is applicable to groups of 15 or more, although you may want to adopt it sooner if you don't have someone around who cares to track dates.

Effective Communication

Much of our work is collaborative, requiring coordination between teams, organizations, or individuals. In other words – meetings! A distributed workplace introduces a new set of opportunities and challenges for how your team can use meetings, check-ins, presentations, and brainstorms to advance your organization's objectives. We've catalogued our best distributed communications principles and practices here. We strongly encourage you to adopt these as companywide practices.

Pick Your Battles (and Your Meetings) Nobody likes poorly run meetings or too many meetings, but because we are members of a distributed team, bumping into each other in the hallway is not an option. Thus, we tend to have frequent meetings. The good news is that investing the time to figure out how to do meetings well has incredible payoffs for any team, whether it's distributed, hybrid, or in-person.

Regularly Scheduled Meetings   Well-defined meetings can make your team more efficient. The following are meetings that should be implemented at a regular cadence for your distributed team. Please also note that deploying all of these meetings at once will be overwhelming. Pick one to start with and then gradually add, over the course of weeks or months, others that are relevant to your team. This approach will yield maximum benefits without the risk of notable eye-rolling.

The Retrospective   The function of a retrospective (commonly called a *retro*) is to get the whole team talking about what's going well and what isn't in a curated and constructive fashion. The output of the retrospective is a set of actions that are to be completed by the next retrospective with the goal of improving the team. See Chapter 3 to learn more.

Interval Planning   Interval planning (also called sprint planning) is how your team decides what it's going to do on a week-by-week basis. This is where the team accepts work from the inbox/tasklist, schedules work in their backlog, gets business context from their lead or manager, and sets up their goals for the interval (or sprint).

As is the case with retros, there are different ways to run interval planning. We like to start with a general overview or a review of news for the week, followed by a run-through of any work in progress, followed by inbox processing until the inbox is empty or the hour is up.

Truss believes strongly in a one-week interval and generally finds that higher-performing teams operate on a one- or two-week interval.

Daily Standup   The standup is a 15-minute meeting that happens once per working day. It is a space where team members can share what they've worked on and what they're currently working on, raise issues that are blocking progress on their work, and do tactical planning.

Although this meeting isn't required, it's extremely useful with new teams so folks get used to how to report progress and catch missed expectations early. It is also useful in crisis scenarios, when the lay of the land is constantly changing and a weekly check-in cadence isn't viable. If video chat standups aren't possible, your team can hold asynchronous standups, where folks share their progress and blockers via chat, typically at a preappointed time.

Manager and Report 1:1   Every member of your team should have a scheduled, one-hour meeting with their manager that happens at least every two weeks. This isn't a status meeting, but rather time for each person to have an in-depth discussion with their manager about problems, planning, career progress, and other issues. The individual, not their manager, owns the meeting and runs the agenda.

Good Meetings, Bad Meetings, and How to Tell the Difference
We've all been in bad meetings. No matter how great your crew is, bad meetings waste time and can degrade the culture you've worked hard to build. Once you've decided which meetings make sense for you and an appropriate cadence, you must determine how to get the most out of those meetings.

Is This Meeting Worth Having?   Any scheduled event has the potential to disrupt a coworker's flow. In the worst-case scenario, meetings can feel like a huge waste of time. In the best case, they often require context switching. Before calling a meeting, take a moment to think about whether you actually need someone to do something synchronously with you or whether working asynchronously could accomplish the same goal.

When It Makes Sense to Have a Meeting   An unnecessary meeting is a bad meeting. It is hard, however, to know the difference and a bad meeting for you may be great for someone else. Here are situations that we think require a meeting:

- **When something can't be decided on asynchronously.** We try to coordinate as many conversations as possible using a messaging app (for example, Slack, Hive, or Hangouts). This practice allows team members to make simple, nonurgent requests that their coworkers can address when time allows. Online, text-based communication doesn't work for everyone, though, especially if multiple parties need to provide input at the same time, or if you're working on a single document that requires collaborative editing to move forward.

- **When important nuances of conversation could be lost.** In certain situations, the team could benefit from multiple mediums of communication – visual, verbal, and physical – happening concurrently. In these cases, call a meeting instead of communicating asynchronously.

- **When something has been decided, but there needs to be a group status update to move on to other things.** Sometimes you may be able to make a decision via text-based communication, but your team may have outstanding concerns or anxieties. A meeting may be the best and most efficient way to quell your team's fears. By holding a recap meeting, you can ensure that everyone is aware of the decisions that have been made, allowing the team to collectively move on to the next phase of the project.

- **To build team cohesion.** Asynchronous communication with occasional one-on-ones just doesn't keep the whole team connected at an optimal level. Sometimes the team needs to get together to learn from each other and to realize just how aligned they already are.

When You Shouldn't Have a Meeting   Some meetings do more to waste time than to move a project forward, which leads to a lot of frustrated team members. Here are some signs you're not having a meaningful meeting:

- **You're reading together.** There are some people who don't read the materials they're supposed to in advance of a meeting. If that's the case, they are not ready to be in that meeting. They should leave or the meeting should be rescheduled.

- **Only one person is speaking.** If you want to give a presentation, own it! Recognize that presentations are just as easily ingested in video or audio recording formats. Don't disrupt people's workflows because you want to hold court.

- **You're hearing people talking about things they already know.** This isn't a meeting, it's a panel discussion. The same principles apply as listening to one person speak. If you're not up to adapting your topic to your audience's needs, or actively helping them learn something new, make a recording and distribute it. The knowledge is still useful, but the disruption of other people's workflows is not.

The Meeting Itself You've determined that you need to schedule a meeting – excellent work! Your next step should be to make your meeting matter. Before holding the meeting, take some time to ensure that it won't go off the rails. We take the following steps to make sure our meetings are as productive as possible.

Create an Agenda Building an agenda is the most important part of the meeting. If you can't explain your agenda, revise it. If you want to hang out with co-workers, cool, but don't pull people out of their workday. Follow these steps to create a solid agenda:

- **Establish a concrete outcome for the meeting**. You should be able to summarize your desired outcome in one sentence. Once you've settled on your outcome, make it the name of the meeting (on your calendar invite) or explicitly state it at the top of the call.
- **Identify your requirements and blockers**. What needs to happen for your team to realize your outcome? Can any of the people at your meeting identify blockers to reach this outcome?
- **Create a strategy for tackling challenges**. Once you've identified your endpoints, list concrete steps you can take to move the group from point A to point B.
- **Identify the leaders who can push a project forward**. In general, avoid asking a decision maker to facilitate your meeting. The meeting facilitator should focus on running the meeting, and the decision maker(s) should focus on solving the problem at hand.

Time Management   Time management is extremely difficult to get right, especially if you're new to facilitating meetings. Here are some ways to effectively manage meeting time:

- **Pad for time.** People will show up late. Decide how long you're willing to wait for stragglers and stick to your time limit. Keep in mind that waiting wastes everyone else's time and sets a bad precedent. People will show up on time more often if they know *you* start on time.

- **A/V will break.** If you are dependent on music, sound, slides, or guest presenters, test or rehearse your A/V and your transitions. Show up early to troubleshoot if you have any A/V concerns.

- **Leave time for questions.** Folks will want to dig into topics that matter – set aside some time for questions and discussion. Leave time to open and close. Rituals matter!

Facilitating   You've done all the work, you're ready to try out your well-crafted agenda, and people are on the call or at the table, hopefully on time. What do you do now?

Set expectations around communication. First, demonstrate respect for each attendee, their time, and their attention. If discussion points are timebound, and they should be, then have a hard time stop. Likewise, start and end when you say you are going to. At the end of the meeting, if you haven't addressed any critical points, set a follow-up meeting or use your messaging service for an asynchronous update.

Another key practice is to follow the Rules of 1:

- **Make one point and pass the proverbial mic to someone else.** This balances the conversational load among all participants, which means that everyone will have a chance to be heard.

- **One diva, one mic.** Only one person should speak at a time. This practice prevents people from talking over each other and makes it easier for folks dialing in to hear the conversation. It also gives equal attention to all speakers.
- **Speak 1/Nth of the time.** If you're quiet, know people want to hear from you. If you're gregarious, dial back a bit to make room for others.

You won't be able to follow all of these rules at once, but they provide a useful framework for effective meetings. If someone from your team habitually violates these guidelines, give them a gentle nudge to help them course correct.

Using Decision Records (DRs)

The practice of decision records comes out of engineering playbooks, and it is a means of documenting key decisions. We use a set template:

- Title (what is the decision)
- Status (drafted, pending, done)
- Deciders (names)
- Submitters (names)
- Date
- Problem We're Trying to Solve
- Considered Options (usually at least two other options)
- Decision Outcome
- Positive and Negative Consequences
- How Do We Undo This Decision?

The primary value is making decisions traceable. How many of us have spent frustrating time in a futile search for why a decision was made? Decision records are a lightweight system to avoid that problem.

In 2021, we noticed that we weren't using DRs for strategic decisions, like, "Should we create a budget for face-to-face Truss meetups to help people stay connected if we don't have our offsite this year?" We're experimenting with using a variant of DRs, where we are explicit about Type 1 and Type 2 decision-making and include the assessment of when the risk increases if we don't make a decision. As always, the goal is a repeatable process that reduces the work that any individual must endure.

Implementing Auxiliary Groups

We use different forms of internal groups to cover ongoing activities, solve specific problems, develop expertise, or foster community. This is also an important employee engagement strategy that increases alignment, reduces blind spots, and increases employee engagement on important companywide objectives:

- **Working group:** A working group is a temporary group that works together to meet an objective. An example is the offsite working group.

- **Committees:** These are "forever" working groups; they cover activities that the organization has to do to function. An example is our compensation committee.

- **Guilds:** These are groups that are focused on a specific topic or area of expertise, focused on deepening that expertise on behalf of the company. An example is our facilitation guild.

- **Affinity groups:** These are groups formed around a need for solidarity around identity and thriving in a world that has marginalized different groups. An example is our Black Slack channel.

Each of these groups is part of Declare It Center, because they are people-focused infrastructure that enables the entire company to benefit from their work. As you saw in Chapters 2 and 3, the salary transparency group plays a big role in making our decisions better. Our facilitation guild is a big source of experiments to improve our meeting hygiene, our weekly all-hands meeting, and our quarterly stakeholders meeting.

Affinity groups around neurodiversity, race, and gender identification play a role in ensuring our diverse company continues to create spaces for everyone to thrive. Auxiliary groups that seem like just "fun" – dogs, movie club, gardening, food – also carry seeds of the Truss culture. For instance, when a new Trussel joins, we ask them to share on our Slack channel a few of their interests, their location, and the project they are joining. Other folks will respond with auxiliary groups and the Slack channels they can join that reflect their interests. This is a great way to be welcomed and reminds new employees there are probably multiple places for them to be their best selves. These outcomes are the result of the intentional decisions of how we use auxiliary groups.

Putting Your Money Where Your Mouth Is: Investing in Connection

We subscribe to the Good Jobs Strategy approach (goodjobsinstitute.org). In a nutshell, this strategy advises organizations to avoid underspending in areas that support employee effectiveness as much as possible within their budgets.

This approach is both an act of trust with your employees and a smart investment. Here is a selection of these investments we make at Truss.

Offer a One-Time Home Office Budget   It's important for all employees, collocated or distributed, to have work environments that are copacetic to creativity and productivity. Your organization should support your employees by making home-office improvements that help them work. This means making sure that your employees are working in spaces that are physically comfortable, allow them to concentrate, enable them to communicate well, and facilitate their best work.

Truss grants each new employee $1,000 to spend on any home office supplies they need, including peripherals, monitors, chairs, ergonomic support, desks, and so on. This does not include things like monthly internet (your employees probably already have that), coffee to drink at home, or other aesthetic touches.

Pay for the Good Headphones   Whether your employees work from a home office, a co-working space, or a coffee shop, you want them to be able to focus on their work without noisy distractions. We recommend establishing a dedicated headphone budget for each employee and authorizing your employees to purchase high-end noise-canceling headphones.

The Truss "standard" is the Bose QC-35ii, which retails for around $350, but there are others that are of similar quality that present different trade-offs. For example, sales personnel or people continually on meetings may want to consider over-ear, noise-canceling headphones with a boom mic for better fidelity.

Provide an Employee Effectiveness Budget Truss has always had an expense policy that allows employees to spend Truss funds on things that improve their effectiveness – for example, software, laptop accessories, or other productivity-boosting tools. These purchases are completely within the employee's discretion so long as what's being purchased has a reasonable relationship to making the employee more effective (e.g., having coffee while working from a cafe, or purchasing a monthly subscription to a software tool that only that employee uses).

It may seem counterintuitive or strange to pay for things like café visits or fancy headphones, but this investment in effectiveness pays substantial dividends, not just for Truss but for many other companies. In fact, before adopting this approach, we did our homework and found that other distributed companies had similar mechanisms. In particular, we were influenced by GitLab's policy on spending company money, which we encourage you to review.[8]

We tried the employee effectiveness budget, and it works. This was especially useful after the pandemic reduced all connection from March 2020 through August 2021. We had to cancel three in-person offsites, which are even more critical for distributed companies to stay connected. Recognizing the drain that disconnection had on everyone, we added additional monthly funds to encourage people to get together in person. Co-working for a week, sharing a coffee, or having a weekend brunch in the park recharges connections. It is a fantastic investment, whether you are hybrid or fully remote.

Encourage Employees to Practice Discretionary Acts of Kindness
We encourage our employees to use their effectiveness budgets to do nice things for other Trussels. Over the years, we've sent each other stickers, coffee cups, and yarn. Encouraging, not merely allowing, employees to treat their coworkers to small acts

of kindness directly helps members of our distributed team bond and increases team morale.

Implement Managerial Review of Expenses   To ensure that no one takes an unreasonable interpretation of "effectiveness" or "home office," Truss has managers review and approve all expenses. To date, these budgets have not been abused. We more often than not have to remind people to use them, and we expect that you will experience the same.

It Is Worth It?   Spending $1,350 on each employee during their initial onboarding, plus an employee effectiveness budget may seem like a lot. However, Truss saves well over a million dollars each year that would have been paid in renting offices. For a company of over 120 people, there's ample opportunity to invest that savings in training, offsites, and other supporting systems to help our employees thrive.

Moreover, following a distributed model means that Truss can hire anyone, anywhere, so long as they have a strong internet connection. This has provided a key recruiting advantage, as many Trussels could not work for us if we required them to be physically present in a San Francisco office. The bottom line is better employees for less money – not too shabby.

Staying Healthy Is a Practice

One of the biggest apprehensions we've heard from clients and other companies is the impact of shifting the patterns of office work to a home environment. Healthy work habits are hard to manage when everyone is at the same location. By this logic, it seems that promoting healthy work habits across a distributed team must be even more difficult. This simply isn't true, although cultivating healthy habits outside of a physical office requires forethought and deliberate choices. Here are some principles that have worked for us.

Sick Leave   As of the writing of this playbook, COVID is expected to get worse before it gets better. Based on the research we've done, a person infected with COVID may need between two and four weeks to recover. For this reason, your sick leave policy may be one of the first things your leadership team should check and evaluate.

Truss's approach to sick leave is simple: We want you to be healthy, stay healthy, and keep your family and colleagues healthy. Let your team know, stay home, rest, and see your doctors when it's needed. We have your back. This is not just Truss's approach to COVID, but rather, it has been our stance on sick leave since our first employees joined the team.

That said, we've been surprised that many Trussels default to "working through sickness," no matter how many times their colleagues and managers tell them to not work if they are sick. We've often had to encourage people who are clearly unwell to take the day off.

As you implement your new sick-leave policy, your employees may need a bit of time to get used to it as they deprogram themselves of unhealthy work habits. Until your employees realize that you value their health and won't punish them for taking care of themselves, you'll need to reiterate this message.

Our advice to leaders: Make it easy for your people to take care of themselves. You're building a resilient organization; expect to repeat the message and model the behavior you want to see.

Taking Breaks Employees of distributed companies may initially find it difficult to block off time to eat, take a break, or recharge. Some people may fail to identify that breaks are part of a healthy work habit. However, taking breaks is an important part of sustaining a daily pace of production according to lots of science and our own experience.

We encourage you to experiment with different ways of getting your employees to take breaks and to share success stories with the rest of your company. Here are examples from two Trussels about how to build breaks into every workday:

- "I now try to take a 5- to 10-minute break every two hours. My version of a break is to physically move to another spot and engage my brain in something else: reading a book, making tea, doing some stretches, etc. I've found this practice really does help me re-center, and it's way easier to do things in two-hour blocks than six-hour blocks."

- "I use the Time Out app to remind me to take breaks (although I don't always listen . . .). I also put musical instruments near my desk and when I see them, I'm reminded to play a song and stop working for a bit. I also avoid taking breaks that involve staring into the catacombs of social media. I also used to break up my day by going for a run or doing some other exercise for 30 minutes."

Implementing break times across a distributed team can be harder than it seems. We encourage you to record what works for various team members and share these practices broadly.

Boundaries Between Work and Not Work When you're working from home, it's easy to do "just one more thing" and wind up grinding away for longer than you'd intended. When there isn't the fast train to catch home or a deadline to beat the traffic, the boundary between work and not-work can be fluid. Diffuse boundaries between work and not-work can lead to negative outcomes. Our observations, which are substantiated by researchers, show that work quality degrades above 40–50 hours per week.[9]

Moving to a distributed model is an opportunity to set or reset your expectations for work so that you and your company can be effective and resilient. At Truss, we encourage our employees to work about 40 hours per workweek. We recognize that at times, employees will need to work more than 40 hours, and we have policies in place to prevent burnout, including our surge protection below.

Surge Protection Time   Whatever your company's average work week, there will be times when deadlines, unexpected incidents, customer demands, or other issues require your team to work long hours. At Truss, we call these circumstances a *surge*.

As a policy, Truss keeps a sustainable pace of work. We want our employees to maintain their health and sanity after a surge. To enable this, we ask employees to take time off to recover (this time off is known as *surge time*). If employees work more than 40 hours in a week – be it due to client-related travel, long days, or tight deadlines – we ask employees to let their managers know about the overage and ask for surge time. It's each employee's responsibility to determine how much surge time they need to fully recover, and we trust that employees won't abuse this policy (to date, they haven't). Because the primary intent of surge time is to help employees maintain a healthy attitude and work – life balance, we do not allow surge days to be used as floating holidays.

Picking the Right Tools

To function successfully in a distributed setting, each team needs to have alignment around expectations, communications, and tools. These are the three building blocks of remote collaboration. Unfortunately, due to COVID, many of you are building this infrastructure on the fly. We hope that you can gain inspiration from the groundwork we've done and adapt our practices and tools to suit your organization's needs.

Someone once said, "Don't let your tools become your process." This is key advice for working in a distributed office because you will, by necessity, rely on imperfect tools. A thorough review of the different types of tools is beyond the scope of this document, but we can tell you which tools we use for what purposes.

Security Tools Having a distributed practice requires different security measures than a physical office. We sincerely, truly, and deeply do not want to be giving you security advice. Seriously. But we have found three tools to be sufficiently useful that we recommend you consider using them or their competitors.

Password Manager We use a password manager to ensure that we use strong, unique passwords for all of our tools. We went with 1Password, but there are other password management tools that work just as well (e.g., Last Pass, Keeper). Your organization should strongly consider adopting one and deploying it to every single device, including laptops, phones, and tablets.

Device Management Truss maintains our devices via a tool called Kandji. This means if we need to give device images to a client, or if we lose a laptop or a password, we'll be able to respond. We literally had a laptop stolen out from the hands of one of our employees and were able to remotely wipe the drive minutes later. The device management software that is best for your organization is highly dependent on your situation and features change year over year (Windows vs. Mac, remote vs. office, for example) so we can't make blanket recommendations.

Backup   We use Backblaze to back up our computers. It runs in the background and incrementally backs up files to cloud storage. Installation requires some manual configuration, but we can recover full images quickly. These benefits are definitely worth the effort. Again, the best software for your company will depend on your particular configuration and needs.

Team Chat Apps   We value security. We also value open and transparent communication. Team chat apps are superior to email in every way by these standards. Specifically, team chat apps are walled gardens where you control who has an account (and thus can speak to your employees) and who does not. This eliminates the risks of viruses, malware, spam, and phishing that are prevalent across email. Also, as explained below, channels allow anyone to have discussions in public and semi-public forums that eliminate the spamminess of reply-all chains.

There are many chat apps that your organization can choose, from Microsoft Teams to Google Chat. We picked Slack because of its many integrations, its security, and its price. Just because Slack works for us doesn't mean it will be the best option for your company.

How Team Chat Works   Slack and most other chat apps are organized into "channels" that define subject matters. Anyone can join these channels, and messages posted in a given channel will be viewable to all channel members. Channels can be public, meaning any employee (and clients/vendors/contractors who have permission) can be in them. They can also be private – limited to specific teams or individuals. Chat apps also allow you to direct message (DM) any particular person so you can have a private exchange with them.

Truss defaults to every channel being public unless there is an explicit reason why a channel should be private (one example is our legal channel, whose membership is limited to the executive team and the general counsel). Maintaining public channels offers a dramatic increase in transparency over email; unlike email, public channels let people opt into – or out of – conversations as they wish. Public channels also serve as a searchable record of conversations, helping preserve institutional knowledge.

How We Slack   Trussels can join whichever channels they wish, but they are responsible for being able to receive critical communications and thus must be in a few channels. For example, if we hired a new engineer to work on the Happy Magic Fun Ball team, we would expect them to join their team's dedicated channel, another that is shared with the client, the engineering channel, and any other channel directly related to their professional development and project-specific updates.

In addition, we add every new Trussel to a suite of general-interest channels, including:

- **general**: Where we share all-company updates.
- **random**: Not sure where it goes? It goes here! (This is also where we chatter during our weekly all-hands meetings, instead of in the Zoom chat.)
- **onboarding**: Questions and improvement suggestions for onboarding.

- **love**: Share love for your fellow coworkers and the things they do. This is a great place to call out the awesome things that you see someone do that would otherwise be invisible to the rest of the company.

- **wins**: A channel where folks list successes, large and small.

- **announcements**: Must-read messages for everyone at the company. Discussions about announcements take place in other channels, typically #general or #random.

- **rage_cage**: Where folks vent frustrations IN ALL CAPS.

- **celebrations**: A channel where our birthday bot shares notifications of members' birthdays and start dates.

Team members can join various affinity group channels – channels for groups formed around shared gender, race, or other identities. Team members must request admission to affinity-group channels. Requests are approved by existing channel administrators. This helps keep the channel focused and creates a safe space for its members.

Trust us on this: You will have a lot of channels. After a certain point, your people cannot be expected to keep up with every conversation. Here are some suggestions we share with all employees:

- It's okay to mute channels.

- It's okay to leave channels. This should not be taken personally. Pop back in if you want to see what's going on.

- It's fine to join a channel to ask a question about that topic – #accounting or #bizops, for example – and leave once you get your answer.

- You aren't required to always be available on chat.

- We use a default Do Not Disturb schedule, but you can set one that works better for you.

- Nobody is required to immediately respond to every message, especially outside of normal working hours. Keep this in mind both when you ping someone else and when you are pinged.

- We consider it a best practice to respond to DMs by the end of the workday.

- Slack is not the best channel for emergency communications. Use the phone or texting when it's critical to get hold of someone.

- Some of us use multiple Slack workspaces (Truss, client, etc.). You can turn off unread notifications for the Truss workspace if that helps you focus on client work. If you're sharing a message of high importance, disseminate it across multiple channels. This way, everyone on the team can stay on the same page.

Videoconferencing Software   As a fully distributed company, we rely heavily on videoconferencing software for our meetings. This system has worked out pretty well for us, despite some initial bumps. In particular, we learned that if one person is remote, then the entire meeting should be held via video-conference. By requiring that everyone participates in a meeting using the same tools and in the same digital environment, we enable everyone to have the same expectations for how the meeting will proceed. This has resulted in more equitable meetings, more inclusions, and better participation.

As is the case with team chat apps, there are many vendors in this market, like Microsoft Teams to Mmmhmm (from the founder of Evernote). Truss went with Zoom because its product had the fewest glitches and best integrations back in 2012. Since then, we feel that Zoom has only gotten better, but your organization may prefer to use another videoconferencing software.

How We Zoom   Spending a little time setting up Zoom helps make a good experience for you and your co-workers:

- When you set up your Zoom account, assign scheduling privileges to scheduling helpers or executive assistants so they can add or remove meetings on your schedule.

- Integrate Zoom into your Google calendar to make it easier to schedule videoconferences. We are also fans of the Zoom browser plugin that adds Zoom details to Google Calendar invites.

- If possible, use dual monitors. This will let you see a video of folks on one screen and share your other screen. Unfortunately, you will almost certainly find that Zoom puts the screens on the opposite monitors you want it to. Every. Darn. Time.

- Go into Zoom settings and uncheck "Prompt a confirmation before leaving a meeting" so you can eliminate that bit of awkwardness where you've said goodbye but then have to look for the "exit meeting" prompt.

- Some people like to turn on the "Remind me" setting, which lets Zoom give you a notification of an upcoming meeting if you have the Zoom desktop app running in the background.

- Unless you are using a separate push-to-talk system (you probably aren't – see below), apply the following settings:
  - Check "Mute microphone when joining a meeting." This will prevent you from interrupting an in-progress meeting (and will generally help you avoid embarrassment).
  - Check "Press and hold SPACE key to temporarily unmute yourself" – SPACE is easier to find than the unmute button.

- Check "Turn off my video when joining a meeting." This will allow you to gather yourself before entering a meeting space, preventing potentially embarrassing moments.

- If you use the same email account for both Zoom and Slack, you can type /zoom in Slack to generate a quick join link. This is super-useful for ad hoc meetings.
- Add your pronouns to your Zoom handle at set up. Doing this prevents confusion and normalizes inclusion.

When you're in a meeting, follow these helpful tips:

- Use the Zoom chat feature only for on-topic discussions. If you'd like to speak, type "hand" into the chat box. The presenter or facilitator can then walk through the hands in sequence. We've also found it useful to type "response" when you want to respond directly to something that someone else has said. Typing "response" allows the facilitator or presenter to "jump the stack" and call on you to respond, thereby allowing discussion to flow. Zoom does have a "raise hand" function, but we find it difficult to see and prefer just to use the chat.
- Banter can be a really positive contribution to any meeting, especially presentations. It also can be exceptionally distracting. The host should decide if they want banter, and, if they do, then they should make a thread in your team chat app – not Zoom – for banter. This mulleted approach allows business upfront in Zoom, with a party in the back on Slack.
- Full Screen mode is nice, except that it transforms the chat box into a floating window, which always seems to be in the way. Instead of using Full Screen mode, double-click the window title bar so that the window grows to fill the screen (a subtle difference, granted). This keeps the chat box as a bar on the side of the video panel, minimizing distractions.
- To be able to see up to 49 participants in each meeting, go to the video settings and check the box for "Display up to

49 participants per screen in Gallery View." Being able to see all of the participants on a call helps build connections and can minimize confusion.

Without establishing shared expectations and a coherent communication framework, your tools will be instruments of chaos. What tooling you use doesn't matter as much as establishing clear expectations and methods of communication. We strongly encourage you to define your expectations and communication strategy before you concern yourself with tooling. We also want to acknowledge that many tools exist for any particular use case. For example, for videoconferencing, you could choose to use Skype, Google Hangouts, Zoom, or any of their numerous competitors. Which tool you choose is less important than clarity on what you are trying to achieve and how team members should use the tool.

Interior Practices

The following are Interior practices that you can try on your own. There are too many examples to be comprehensive, so I included three exercises that require almost no setup and can be done at any time. These will help you practice meditation, learning from the body and discovering purpose, three of the key themes from Chapter 4 that will help prepare you to make better decisions under uncertainty.

Exercise: Walking Meditation

Walking is an accessible activity for many people, and it happens to be a great opportunity for learning from your body. For readers for whom walking is not accessible, choose your method by which you physically move through the world. Walking meditations take an activity that we normally do on autopilot and turn it into a conscious exploration. The directions are simple, and you can do it in your backyard, around your block, or on your favorite trail.

To start, give yourself space for about twenty paces of normal walking. Walk normally for 20 steps, turn, and return to your original spot. Now that you have the range, pause. Take four normal inhales and exhales, without exertion, but with calm awareness. You might already notice that your inhales or exhales are different lengths. Then begin walking, one step for each inhale, one step for each exhale. Inhale-step, exhale-step. Feels super-slow and weird, right? That's okay, notice whatever you're experiencing, without judgment. When you reach the end of 20 steps, turn and go back to your original spot. Keep this going for 10 minutes to start, then try 20 minutes.

There are many valuable experiences to notice in this simple exercise. You might notice your pace getting slower or faster. You might find yourself saying, "What am I supposed to be doing?" Or "What's the point if we're not going anywhere?" The point is to be curious about any and all of it. It's an experiment with our bodies, and just like the iterations in the previous chapters, each step is a new opportunity to notice something new. I got curious about how my heel hit the ground. I got curious when my careful foot placement made me wobbly because the ground was uneven. I noticed that my hands and forearms grew tense when I was bored and wanted to stop. On one particular walking meditation, I started to hear buzzing, and noticed there was a wonderful group of bees, working hard on the flowering fruit tree that I had walked past, oblivious, for the past 15 minutes.

The gift of this walking – or any simple movement practice – is that it doesn't require equipment or a gym. One of my favorite days in San Francisco was doing a three-hour walking meditation from North Beach to the Mission. I didn't take one breath per step (or I might still be walking), but after practice, I could slip into a calm, aware ease and observe the city with new eyes and learn from my body when I was reacting to things. Isn't that what we're trying to practice as leaders – awareness, insight, and curiosity?

Exercise: Learning from the Body

Here's a quick test: Can you name how you are feeling in this moment? Can you identify where in your body that feeling is located? Did you notice if you were breathing steadily, or did you hold or stop breathing for moment? Might you have a physical tic, like bouncing your knee, that gets activated when you read about physical pain? Your unconscious mind sends signals via the body faster than the conscious mind can articulate. Learning how to read your reactions to stress, uncertainty, and discomfort is a valuable skill.[10]

Exercise: Fear of Missing In

There was a period in my mid-twenties when I was enduring my first major heartbreak and trying to reach out to friends with patient ears and seasoned advice.

Sitting on the floor, propped against my cheap box spring, I called my friend to talk about how to redevelop my sense of direction. I didn't know how to date, how to stay focused at work, or how to have a sense of direction. I thought he'd give me advice to make new friends, try new hangouts, or recommend a career book.

"Here's what you do," he said with Wall-Street-banker directness: "If you're invited to a party, go early. Make the rounds, connect with your friends, have one beer. Then leave early, no later than 9–9:30." He paused. "The next step is the key. When you go home, don't turn on the TV, don't turn on the stereo, don't even open a book. Do nothing that requires you to consume information. Play your flute, drum, write, draw, cook . . . any activity that is creative."

Then came the mic drop. "That's where your dreams are."

I looked at my newly barren walls and came up with my first real purpose statement. *Create more than you consume.*

I hear a lot of people talk about FOMO, Fear of Missing Out. My favorite antidote to this craving is something a friend told me in my thirties. "No matter where you are, there are at least 10 things going on at the exact same time *that are way cooler*. Let it go and enjoy the present."

My urgency about finding purpose is not FOMO, it's about FOMI, Fear of Missing In. I don't want to miss "the heart's longing" because I am looking outward. The practice of leaving early, going home, and creating *something* will bring you closer to your inner purpose.

Appendix: Further Resources

Here are some further resources that I didn't mention in the book:

Brown, Brene. *Daring Greatly* (Avery, 2012). http://www.amazon.com/Daring-Greatly-Courage-Vulnerable-Transforms/dp/1592407331.

Burkeman, Oliver. *The Antidote: Happiness for People Who Can't Stand Positive Thinking* (New York: Farrar, Straus, and Giroux, 2012). http://www.amazon.com/The-Antidote-Happiness-Positive-Thinking/dp/1480527300.

Byrne, Monica. "An artist compiled all her rejections in an 'anti-resume.' Here's what can be learned from failure." *The Washington Post*, August 8, 2014. https://www.washingtonpost.com/posteverything/wp/2014/08/08/an-artist-compiled-all-her-rejections-in-an-anti-resume/.

Grant, Adam. *Think Again: The Power of Knowing What You Don't Know* (New York: Viking, 2021).

Saravathy, Saras. "What makes entrepreneurs entrepreneurial?" *For submission to Harvard Business Review, revised June* (2001). http://www.khoslaventures.com/wp-content/uploads/What_makes_entrepreneurs_entrepreneurial.pdf.

Prof. Saras Sarasvathy writes: The most valuable skill of a successful entrepreneur . . . isn't "vision" or "passion." Rather, it's the ability to adopt an unconventional approach to learning: an improvisational flexibility not merely about which route to take towards some predetermined objective, but also a willingness to change the destination itself. This is a flexibility that might be squelched by rigid focus on any one goal. The effectualists include the cook who scours the fridge for leftover ingredients. "Start with your means. Start taking action, based on what you have readily available: what you are, what you know and who you know."

Notes

Preface

1. Ellen McGirt's Race Ahead newsletter for *Forbes* is a consistent, prolific (nearly daily) resource for the intersection of business, race, and culture filtered with her keen journalist's eye.
2. Ellen McGirt, Why Employers Need to Talk about the Police Shootings of Black People, Fortune, July 7, 2016.
3. Kim Scott, *Radical Candor* (St. Martin's Press, 2019).

Introduction

1. Allen C. Bluedorn, *Scientific Management* (comprising Shop Management, The Principles of Scientific Management, Testimony before the Special House Committee, New York: Harper, 1947), *Academy of Management Review* 11, no. 2 (April 1, 1986).
2. Mark Hamilton, The ad that changed advertising, Medium.com, March 20, 2015, https://medium.com/@marathonmilk; Bob Garfield, Ad Age Advertising Century: The Top 100 Campaigns AdAge (March 2, 1999), https://adage.com/article/special-report-the-advertising-century/ad-age-advertising-century-top-100-campaigns/140918.
3. Samuel Arbesman, Overcomplicated, *Portfolio*, Reprint edition (June 20, 2017).

4. Peter Ho and Adrian W. J. Kuah, "Governing for the Future," *Prism* 5, no. 1 (2014), https://cco.ndu.edu/Portals/96/Documents/prism/prism_5-1/Governing_for_the_future.pdf.

5. Reader, please note that I do none of these things, but I admire those who do.

6. Regarding the planning fallacy, see Daniel Kahneman, *Thinking, Fast and Slow* (New York: Farrar, Straus, and Giroux, 2011), p. 251.

7. Two related perspectives that discuss complexity are from John Allspaw and the fallacies in statistical analysis, Twitter, April 30, 2021, https://twitter.com/allspaw/status/1388156075015381000?s=20.

8. The second is that we do work in teams, not individually, but the cultural remnants of "solo" work still influence the way we think about solving problems. Alan Cooper, Twitter, November 8, 2018, https://twitter.com/mralancooper/status/1060553914209071106.

9. The Agile Manifesto, https://agilemanifesto.org/.

10. A phrase we use at Truss is: "Be Agile, not Do Agile." There is a limit to the codification of Agile, because when Agile becomes just another gate for certification, companies lose sight of the purpose. Don't do this.

11. Eric Ries, *The Lean Startup: How Today's Entrepreneurs Use Continuous Innovation to Create Radically Successful Businesses* (New York: Crown Business, 2011); Steve Blank, *The Four Steps to the Epiphany: Successful Strategies for Products that Win*, 5th ed. (Hoboken, NJ: John Wiley & Sons, 2020).

12. General Stanley McChrystal, Tantum Collins, David Silverman, and Chris Fussell, *Team of Teams: New Rules of Engagement for a Complex World* (New York: Portfolio/Penguin, 2015).

13. BIPOC refers to Black, Indigenous and People of Color. It is an imperfect term to address Black, Indigenous, Latino/a/x, Indian, and Pacific Islander bodies of culture. There are well-reasoned arguments against BIPOC, notably those that the desire to create an inclusive term also erases the specific cultural heritage between and within each group.

14. "Underrepresented minorities" is used here as a reference to US government designations used to make policy, such as the SBA 8(a)

designation. For a software company like Truss, this would include women and Black founders/owners, but in other contexts it would include BIPOC owners as well. While the term may be accurate, it's another imperfect term that emphasizes "otherness" and erases specific context.

15. K. Y. Williams and C. A. O'Reilly III. "Demography and Diversity in Organizations: A Review of 40 Years of Research." *Research in Organizational Behavior* 20 (1998): 77–140.

16. Katherine W. Phillips, Katie A. Liljenquist, Margaret A. Neale, "Is the Pain Worth the Gain? The Advantages and Liabilities of Agreeing with Socially Distinct Newcomers," *Personality and Social Psychological Bulletin* (2008).

17. Katia Savachuk, "Do Investors Really Care About Gender Diversity?" *Stanford Business*, September 17, 2019. Article cites a study by David P. Daniels, Jennifer E. Dannals, Thomas Z. Lys and Margaret A. Neale.

18. Project Include: https://projectinclude.org/.

19. Daniel Kahneman, *Thinking, Fast and Slow* (New York: Farrar, Straus, & Giroux, 2011), p. 20.

20. This is a good meditation practice! However, it's a challenge to do one great breath, much less 30 minutes of attentive breathing.

21. There is a great list in Wikipedia, https://en.wikipedia.org/wiki/List_of_cognitive_biases, but I encourage people to read *Thinking, Fast and Slow* to explore the details of how and why these biases exist.

22. When commentators talk about *intelligence*: *62 percent of praise* was aimed at players with lighter skin tone, *63.33 percent of criticism* was aimed at players with darker skin tone. When commentators talk about work ethic, *60.40 percent of praise* is aimed at players with lighter skin tone. See Danny McLoughlin, Racial bias in football commentary (Study): The pace and power effect, *RunRepeat* (August 6, 2021).

23. Jim Collins and Morten T. Hansen, *Great by Choice: Uncertainty, Chaos, and Luck – Why Some Thrive Despite Them All* (New York: Harper Business, 2011).

24. "Stats and Events," CAL Fire, https://www.fire.ca.gov/stats-events/ and "California Wildfires History and Statistics," Frontline Wildfire Defense, https://www.frontlinewildfire.com/california-wildfires-history-statistics/.

25. Walter B. Cannon, *The Wisdom of the Body* (New York: W.W. Norton & Company, 1932).

26. Shelley E. Taylor, Laura Cousino Klein, Brian P. Lewis, et al., "Biobehavioral Responses to Stress in Females: Tend-and-Befriend, Not Fight-or-Flight," *Psychological Review* 107 (3) (2000): 411–429.

27. These patterns may not be evenly distributed. As we saw earlier, Shelley Taylor's research suggests women are more likely to "tend and friend." I would not be surprised if there was a dimension that tested differences based on race, but I'm unaware of research that tested this yet.

28. Everett Harper, "Company Talk about Police Shootings, as Target and CEO," *Forbes*, May 27, 2020.

29. Center for Advanced Study in Behavioral Sciences, CASBS Summit: The Future of Agency: Transforming the University and City-State, Stanford University. November 30, 2015, https://youtu.be/VJzr85nfxgE CASBS Presentation.

Chapter 1

1. Listen to the album *Segundo*, by Juana Molina. Recorded almost entirely in the *madrugada*, she reflects this time of night with complex soundscapes, suffused in sleep, yet full of wit and reflection in lyrics.

2. *Andy Warhol: A Documentary Film*, directed by Ric Burns, 2006.

3. The Factory was Andy Warhol's studio, but it became a cultural magnet for the avant-garde in New York City, creating and defining cultural trends for the remainder of the decade.

Chapter 2

1. K. Anders Ericsson, Robert Pool, *Peak: Secrets from the New Science of Expertise*, Eamon Dolan/HMH (US) Bodley Head (UK), 2016. Mr. Ericsson appeared on Michael Gervais' podcast, Finding Mastery on Sept. 21, 2016, https://findingmastery.net/anders-ericsson/.

2. Riffing off Maria Konnikova, *The Biggest Bluff: How I Learned to Pay Attention, Master Myself, and Win* (New York: Penguin Press, 2020).

3. Charlan J. Nemeth, *In Defense of Troublemakers, The Power of Dissent in Life and Business* (New York: Basic Books, 2018).

4. Greg Guest, Emily Namey, and Mario Chen, "A simple method to assess and report thematic saturation in qualitative research," *PLOS ONE*, May 5, 2020, https://journals.plos.org/plosone/article?id=10.1371/journal.pone.0232076; Brett Crawford, Todd H. Childes, and Sara R. S. T. A. Elias, "Long interviews in organizational research: Unleashing the power of 'show-and-tell,'" *Journal of Management Inquiry*, May 2020, https://www.researchgate.net/publication/341408602_Long_Interviews_in_Organizational_Research_Unleashing_the_Power_of_Show-and-Tell.

5. Steve Blank, *Successful Strategies for Products that Win*, 5th ed. (Hoboken, NJ: John Wiley & Sons, 2020).

6. Eric Ries, *The Lean Startup: How Today's Entrepreneurs Use Continuous Innovation to Create Radically Successful Businesses* (New York: Crown Business, 2011).

7. Cindy Alvarez, *Lean Customer Development, Lean Customer Development: Building Products Your Customers Will Buy* (O'Reilly, 2017).

8. Everett Harper, "Hidden Figures: One Woman's Fight to Be an IBM Programmer in the 1970s," *Forbes*, May 13, 2018; Melinda Byerley, Jacqueline Harper, *Stayin' Alive in Technology* (October 2, 2019), https://www.stayinaliveintech.com/podcast/2019/s3-e3/jacqueline-harper-shining-star.

9. Amy Moran-Thomas, "How a Popular Medical Device Encodes Racial Bias," *Boston Review*, August 2, 2020, https://bostonreview.net/articles/amy-moran-thomas-pulse-oximeter/; Queenie Wong, "Why Facial Recognition's Racial Bias Problem Is So Hard to Crack, c l net, March 27, 2019, https://www.cnet.com/google-amp/news/why-facial-recognitions-racial-bias-problem-is-so-hard-to-crack/. Interestingly, there are Black entrepreneurs who are dedicated to safety in autonomous driving systems. Aicha Evans, CEO of Zoox, and Tekedra Mawakana, Co-CEO of Waymo are overseeing the development of systems that keep people of all skin colors safe.

10. "Talk story" is one of my favorite things I've learned in writing this book. It is a Hawaiian cultural phrase for communicating and dialogue, but it has much deeper meaning for passing ancestral knowledge verbally through generations. As a Black person steeped in the cultural significance of oral storytelling, I resonated deeply with this concept. You will hear Hawaiians casually say, "Let's talk story" when they want to discuss, dialogue.

11. Benjamin Artz, Amanda H. Goodall, and Andrew J. Oswald, *Do Women Ask?*, Warwick Economics Research Papers, July 2016. https://fortune.com/2016/09/06/women-men-salary-negotiations/.

12. The history and her methods are illustrated in *Citizen Jane: Battle for the City*, Documentary film, 2016, directed by Matt Tyrnauer.

13. Robert Caro, *The Power Broker: Robert Moses and the Fall of New York* (Alfred A Knopf Incorporated, 1974).

14. Charles G. Bennett, "Canal St. Expressway Gets Planning Body's Approval," *The New York Times, February 4, 1960. ISSN 0362-4331.*

15. Jane Jacobs, *The Death and Life of Great American Cities* (Vintage, 1961).

16. Yuliya Parshina-Kottas et al., "Tulsa Race Massacre," *New York Times,* May 24, 2021, https://www.nytimes.com/interactive/2021/05/24/us/tulsa-race-massacre.html.

17. Richard P. Hunt, "Expressway Vote Delayed by City; Final Decision Is Postponed After 6-Hour Hearing," *The New York Times*, December 7, 1962.

18. Liz T. Williams, The worst bushfires in Australia, *Australian Geographic*, November 3, 2011, https://www.australiangeographic. com.au/topics/science-environment/2011/11/the-worst-bushfires-in-australias-history/.
19. Not her real name.
20. Jennifer Kates, Josh Michaud, and Jennifer Tolbert, "Stay at Home Orders to Fight COVID-19 in the United States: The Risks of a Scattershot Approach," KFF, April 5, 2020, https://www.kff.org/ policy-watch/stay-at-home-orders-to-fight-covid19/. This was a recommendation to stay home for people over 60 and underlying health conditions.

Chapter 3

1. Histories of the Highlander Center are here in the Library of Congress, https://www.loc.gov/exhibitions/rosa-parks-in-her-own-words/about-this-exhibition/the-bus-boycott/highlander-folk-school/ and in a column by Charles Blow, *Rosa Parks, Revisited*, Feb 1, 2013. I had the opportunity to sit in the famous circle of rocking chairs at the Highlander Center, where Rosa Parks, Dr. Martin Luther King, and other organizers met. It is a humbling and inspiring experience. Tragically, the Highlander Center burned to the ground in 2019 by arsonists, thought to be white supremacists.
2. "In world" was the common term for meeting in a virtual setting inside of Second Life.
3. We use Slack, Zoom, Google Docs, Pivotal Tracker, and Miro now, but we've cycled everything from Skype, Jira, wikis through Asana. The more important thing is to commit to transparency, then figure out the right tool for your org.
4. *Remote-first* refers to building a company with the core assumption that the employees will not be in the same physical location. People are distributed across multiple sites, whether it's home, coworking spaces, or cafes, and they could be in the same city, or across the globe. I prefer *distributed* because *remote* implies

isolation and our goal is to have people feel connected. However, I use *remote* most frequently in the book because it is in more common usage in 2022.

5. Amy Edmondson, *The Fearless Organization: Creating Psychological Safety in the Workplace for Learning, Innovation, and Growth* (Hoboken, NJ: Wiley, 2018).

6. Gary Klein, Performing a Project Premortem, *Harvard Business Review*, September 2007, https://hbr.org/2007/09/performing-a-project-premortem.

7. Morten Bennedsen, Elena Simintzi, Margarita Tsoutsoura, and Daniel Wolfenzon, Research: Gender Pay Gaps Shrink When Companies Are Required to Disclose Them, *Harvard Business Review* (January 23, 2019), https://hbr.org/2019/01/research-gender-pay-gaps-shrink-when-companies-are-required-to-disclose-them.

8. Patient Protection and Affordable Care Act, Status of CMS Efforts to Establish Federally Facilitated Health Insurance Exchanges, *GAO Highlights*, June 2013, https://www.gao.gov/assets/gao-13-601.pdf.

9. Estimates vary about the total size of the contract. The GAO reported $394M in spending on healthcare.gov from FY 2010-2013, $93.7 of which went to CGI Federal, https://www.cgi.com/en/CGI-selected-build-US-wide-competitive-health-insurance-exchange. Other reports claim total figures as high as $515M, https://nymag.com/intelligencer/2013/10/how-much-did-obamacares-broken-website-cost.html.

10. An assumption based on previous signups for Medicare the previous year. It was a faulty assumption based in a complicated decision framework – relying on "the familiar." However, the website users were different, the service was different, and the publicity and curiosity were easy to predict – if the company had used Move to the Edge methods of hypothesis testing and discovery, https://www.usatoday.com/story/news/nation/2013/10/05/health-care-website-repairs/2927597.

11 "We were seeing 250 queries per second throughput for the entire site at best by November. For comparison, 1000 qps per server is pretty solid, with 250 qps per server being acceptable for most purposes. Healthcare.gov had over 1000 servers for the main site at launch and throughout the initial enrollment period, so it was doing about 1/6 qps per server." Mark Ferlatte.

12. This was an era before remote work processes were accepted. Problems like these reinforced our decision for Truss to go remote-first, while encouraging our clients to do the same.

13. The Standish Group, *Haze*. Copyright © 2015 The Standish Group International, Inc., https://www.standishgroup.com/ sample_research_files/Haze4.pdf, https://standishgroup.com/ sample_research_files/CHAOSReport2015-Final.pdf.

14. This was a common refrain, as seen in this article: David Teather and Jonathan Watts, "End of an Era as Firm That Brought Us the PC Sells Out to Chinese Pretender for $1.75bn," *The Guardian*, December 9, 2004, https://www.theguardian.com/technology/ 2004/dec/09/business.china.

15. Ted Nesi, "Raimondo reaches deal to keep Deloitte running UHIP through 2021," WPRI, March 15, 2019, https://www.wpri .com/news/politics/raimondo-reaches-deal-to-keep-deloitte-running-uhip-through-2021/.

16. Reis Thebault, Paulina Firozi, Brittany Shammas, 58 people died in last week's frigid weather, *Washington Post*, February 21, 2021; Matthew Schwartz, *Texas Won't Reduce $16 Billion in Electricity Charges From Winter Storm*, NPR, March 6, 2021, https://www .npr.org/2021/03/06/974417969/texas-wont-reduce-16-billion-in-electricity-charges-from-winter-storm.

17. Cat Ferguson, "What Went Wrong with America's $44 Million Vaccine Data System?" *Technology Review*, January 30, 2021, https:// www.technologyreview.com/2021/01/30/1017086/ cdc-44-million-vaccine-data-vams-problems/.

18. Sheryl Gay Stolberg, Immunization Expert Accuses C.D.C. and Deloitte of Stealing Her Idea, *New York Times*, Feb 6, 2021, https:// www.nytimes.com/2021/02/06/us/politics/coronavirus-vaccines.html.

19. The playbook can be found at playbook.cio.gov.
20. Not her real name.
21. California wildfires history and statistics, Frontline Wildfire Defense, https://www.frontlinewildfire.com/california-wildfires-history-statistics/.
22. For context, Hurricane Katrina was Level Eight.
23. Daniel Kahneman, *Thinking, Fast and Slow* (New York: Farrar, Straus, and Giroux, 2011).

Chapter 4

1. Lauryn Hill, Doo Wop (That Thing), 1998.
2. K. Anders Ericsson, Robert Pool, Eamon Dolan, Peak, Secrets from the New Science of Expertise, HMH (US) Bodley Head (UK), 2016.
3. Running shoes, without cleats. Translation: you are going to run until every fiber in your body screams STOP!
4. One of the gifts of any performing discipline is that you learn how to deal with making obvious errors that have serious consequences. Playing the wrong note at the wrong time in an orchestra, forgetting your lines in a play, or having an opponent pass the ball between your legs to score a goal are big, obvious, public mistakes – and learning to overcome the emotions that come with it starts at an early age. And yes, I've done all of these.
5. This is a reference to a passage in one of my favorite speeches, by Theodore Roosevelt. Quoted here, with caveats that the term "man" is hella outdated now, but in 1910 it represented humans in general. *"It is not the critic who counts; not the man who points out how the strong man stumbles or where the doer of deeds could have done them better. The credit belongs to the man who is actually in the arena, whose face is marred by dust and sweat and blood; who strives valiantly; who errs, who comes short again and again, because there is no effort without error and shortcoming; but who does actually strive to do the deeds; who knows the great enthusiasms, the great devotions; who spends himself in*

a worthy cause; who at the best knows in the end the triumph of high achievement, and who at the worst, if he fails, at least fails while daring greatly, so that his place shall never be with those cold and timid souls who neither know victory nor defeat." From "Citizenship in a Republic" at the Sorbonne in Paris on April 23, 1910, https://www.theodo reroosveltcenter.org/Learn-About-TR/TR-Encyclopedia/ Culture-and-Society/Man-in-the-Arena.aspx.

6. Special note: I'm not a mental health expert, so specific experiences and practices related to topics like acute anxiety, depression, trauma, and neurodiversity are out of scope for this book. There is a welcome increase in number of resources for those topics, and I encourage readers to find those resources as companions to the practices described here. I am personally grateful to the guides, mentors, therapists, and communities who shared their wisdom and expertise with me over the years, and who have influenced the practices I'm sharing in this book.

7. Thay is an affectionate name for teacher.

8. Thích Nhất Hạnh, *The Miracle of Mindfulness* (Beacon Press, 1975), ISBN 0-8070-1239-4 (Classic edition, 7 February 2008, 9781846041068).

9 Mihaly Csikszentmihalyi, *Flow: The Psychology of Optimal Experience* (New York: Harper and Row, 1990).

10. Johns Hopkins Medical Institutions. "This Is Your Brain on Jazz: Researchers Use MRI to Study Spontaneity, Creativity," *ScienceDaily* (February 28, 2008), www.sciencedaily.com/releases/2008/02/ 080226213431.htm.

11. Competing is about vulnerability. This is the same with taking "blame" while coaching. Good example to follow, https://podcasts. apple.com/us/podcast/flying-coach-with-steve-kerr-and-pete-carroll/id1507792638?i=1000472896879.

12. In basketball, that is 25 points, 10 assists, and 10 rebounds.

13. An early iteration appeared in this article. Everett Harper, "Trouble Sticking to Resolutions? Try Leading with a Purpose Playbook Instead," *Forbes* (January 16, 2018).

14. Robert Hess, "A.I. meets DNA," Statistic Brain Research Institute, https://www.statisticbrain.com/new-years-resolution-statistics/.

15. MeiMei Fox, "How to Discover Your Life Purpose: A Tech Start-Up CEO Shares His Recipe for Success," *Forbes*, July 12, 2016, https://www.forbes.com/sites/meimeifox/2016/07/12/how-to-discover-your-life-purpose-a-tech-start-up-ceo-shares-his-recipe-for-success/2/#24e23b764779.

16. Mei Mei Fox, https://meimeifox.com/ 2021.

17. James Clear, *Atomic Habits* (Avery Publisher, 2018).

18. Ellen Leanse, *The Happiness Hack* (Simple Truths Publisher, 2017).

19. Greg McKeown, *Essentialism: The Disciplined Pursuit of Less* (Currency Publishers, 2014).

20. Mei Mei Fox, https://meimeifox.com/ 2021.

21. Professor Katherine Williams, "How Diversity Makes Us Smarter," *Scientific American*, October 2014, https://www.scientificamerican.com/article/how-diversity-makes-us-smarter/.

22. Mihaly Csikszentmihalyi, *Flow: The Psychology of Optimal Experience* (New York: Harper and Row, 1990).

23. Toni Morrison, Nobel Laureate speech, 1993.

24. My embarrassed self would call it a warning, not a sign. My training is to acknowledge that self, and then tell it to stay quiet.

25. I still own the domain!

26. Andrew Ross Sorkin, "BlackRock Chief Pushes a Big New Climate Goal for the Corporate World," *New York Times*, January 26, 2021, https://www.nytimes.com/2021/01/26/business/dealbook/larry-fink-letter-blackrock-climate.html.

27. "Business Roundtable Redefines the Purpose of a Corporation to Promote an Economy That Serves All Americans," *Business Roundtable*, August 19, 2019, https://www.businessroundtable.org/business-roundtable-redefines-the-purpose-of-a-corporation-to-promote-an-economy-that-serves-all-americans.

28. Roberta Katz, Sarah Ogilvie, Jane Shaw, and Linda Woodhead, *Gen Z, Explained. The Art of Living in a Digital Age* (Chicago: The University of Chicago Press, 2021).

29. Hoya is the nickname for the Georgetown University athletic teams. Duke and Georgetown have a heated sports rivalry. Julie was the captain of the women's basketball team, so this gesture was a REALLY big deal.

Chapter 5

1. There are a lot of anti-racism and/or learning about Whiteness courses. These are a few I've gathered from experts whose judgment and expertise I respect: National Equity Project (https://www.nationalequityproject.org/); Check Your Privilege (https://checkyourprivilege.co/), What Is at Your Core (https://www.whatisatyourcore.com/), Resmaa Menakem (https://www.resmaa.com/).

2. "Certified B Corporations are businesses that meet the highest standards of verified social and environmental performance, public transparency, and legal accountability to balance profit and purpose," https://bcorporation.net/about-b-corps.

3. "Evergreen businesses are led by Purpose-driven leaders with the grit and resourcefulness to build and scale private, profitable, enduring, and market-leading businesses that make a dent in the universe," https://www.tugboatinstitute.com/what-is-evergreen/.

4. And taking notes about how to get more curious myself.

5. While we use she/her, he/him, or they/them categories, unfortunately the EEOC does not. For alignment with their data, we revert to male / female, but continue to use categories that represent our nonbinary employees. I encourage you to do the same.

6. Dinah Wisenberg Brin, "Is Homework for Job Applicants Effective?" *SHRM*, September 10, 2018, https://www.shrm.org/resourcesandtools/legal-and-compliance/employment-law/pages/homework-job-applicants.aspx; Alison Green, "Job Candidates Aren't Free Labor," *Slate*, March 18, 2019, https://slate.com/human-interest/2019/03/job-interview-work-assignments-free-labor.html.

7. "The Ultimate Collection of Recruiting Stats, 2017," Lever.com. These stats are updated annually. There are other sources for recruiting data, and I highly recommend updating these especially in 2021. We've noticed that these stats had some substantial shifts within 90 days.

8. Project Include: https://projectinclude.org/ has a well-researched, pragmatic repository of practices, strategies, and approaches to help organizations become more inclusive. We were part of their first cohort of startups in 2016, and we highly recommend them as a resource.

9. The original open source code for the Slack Bot is from Uk.gov.

Chapter 6

1. Alexander Osterwalder and Yves Pigneur, *Business Model Generation: A Handbook For Visionaries, Game Changers, and Challengers* (Hoboken, NJ: John Wiley & Sons, 2010).

2. Morten Hansen, *Great at Work* (Simon & Schuster, 2018), among others.

3. Instagram, Airbnb, Box and DropBox emerged during this time, for example.

4. Cal Newport, *Deep Work: Rules for Focused Success in a Distracted World* (Grand Central Publishing, 2016).

5. Ed Batista, The Uneasiness of the Open Office," blog, January 3, 2020, https://www.edbatista.com/2020/01/the-uneasiness-of-the-open-office.html.

6. Alan Cooper, widely known as the father of Visual Basic, writes on the evolution of technology and engineering work. See Alan Cooper, Twitter, November 8, 2018, https://twitter.com/mralancooper/status/1060553914209071106.

7. Truss Distributed Playbook, https://guide.truss.works/docs/
   distributed/; Everett Harper, "Remote, Yet Connected: Announcing
   the updated Truss," Truss, April 6, 2020, https://truss.works/blog/
   remote-yet-connected-announcing-the-updated-truss-
   distributed-playbook. Additional authorship from Mark Ferlatte,
   Willow Idlewild, Nick Twyman.

8. Brian Robins, Dale Brown, and Urja Patel, eds., *Spending Company
   Money*, Gitlab Team Handbook, open source (n.d.), https://about.
   gitlab.com/handbook/spending-company-money/.

9. Morten Hansen, "How to Work Smarter, Not Harder, in 2019,"
   blog, January 7, 2019, https://www.mortenhansen.com/how-
   to-work-smarter-not-harder-in-2019/.

10. "Discomfort is a sign something is going right, if we notice it
    sooner and use it, rather than soothe it unconsciously." In Christina
    Harbridge, *Swayed: How to Communicate for Impact* (San Francisco:
    Nothing But the Truth, LLC, 2016).

Index